T0376020

For my father, with whom I shared a deep love of delicious food, words, writing and nature. Until we meet again, fly free my darling dad.

The Wanderlust Kitchen
Samantha Dormehl

First published in the UK and USA in 2025 by
Nourish, an imprint of Watkins Media Limited
Unit 11, Shepperton House,
83–93 Shepperton Road
London N1 3DF

enquiries@nourishbooks.com

Commissioning Editor: Ella Chappell
Project Editor: Brittany Willis
Head of Design: Karen Smith
Original design concept: Samantha Dormehl
Cover Design: nicandlou.com/Karen Smith
Layout: Glen Wilkins/Karen Smith
Production: Uzma Taj
Photography: Samantha Dormehl

A CIP record for this book is available from the
British Library

ISBN: 978-1-84899-431-7 (Hardback)
ISBN: 978-1-84899-432-4 (eBook)

10 9 8 7 6 5 4 3 2 1

Colour reproduction by Rival Colour
Printed in China

Publisher's note
While every care has been taken in compiling
the recipes for this book, Watkins Media
Limited, or any other persons who have been
involved in working on this publication, cannot
accept responsibility for any errors or omissions,
inadvertent or not, that may be found in the
recipes or text, nor for any problems that may
arise as a result of preparing one of these
recipes. If you are pregnant or breastfeeding
or have any special dietary requirements or
medical conditions, it is advisable to consult
a medical professional before following any
of the recipes contained in this book.

Notes on the recipes
Unless otherwise stated:
Use medium fruit and vegetables
Use medium (US large) organic or
free-range eggs
Use fresh herbs, spices and chillies
Use granulated sugar (Americans can
use ordinary granulated sugar when caster
sugar is specified)
Do not mix metric, imperial and US cup
measurements:
1 tsp = 5ml 1 tbsp = 15ml 1 cup = 250ml

nourishbooks.com

MIX
Paper | Supporting
responsible forestry
FSC
www.fsc.org
FSC® C005748

SAMANTHA DORMEHL

The Wanderlust Kitchen

A spiritual guide to healing recipes
from around the world

NOURISH

EAT WELL, LIVE WELL

35

66

88

184

244

286

Contents

JOURNAL ENTRY //

There's nothing quite like
hitting the open road,
throwing caution to the
wind and heading out into
the unknown.

We are innate wanderers.
In ancient times, like
migratory birds, we moved
from place to place guided
by the weather, following
our food source.
We are nomads by nature,
roamers at heart, dreamers
of new adventures.

We crave changing subject

matter to fuel our creative

energy.

To be stagnant is to

accept

your

reality

as finite,

to move is to shed,

to grow,   A small part of your heart

to learn   scattered where your feet

and to give.   have walked, lovingly left for

                                  someone else to find. …

Baja California Sur, Mexico, shot on a Sony a6500 with a Mitakon Zhongyi fixed 35mm lens

Food is Medicine

That first moment I looked into your eyes at only two weeks old, in the goat shed in the foothills of the Sierra Nevada mountains, California, I just knew that you would be a part of our lives forever. It was similar to the feeling I had when I first laid eyes on Samuel, but we'll get to that later.

You, my sweet polar bear, were the only pup out of your six brothers and sisters who stared right into my soul and said, "We've spent lifetimes together, I'm here to guide you through this one." Samuel felt the same way and we admitted to each other later that day that although our circumstances were far from perfect for adopting a dog, we were in love.

And with that you got sick, and we were told you had parvovirus, that all your littermates were likely to contract it and your chances of survival were slim. We took you home and cared for you night and day for a week, giving you a drip three times a day, antibiotics and all the plant magic we could find, from activated charcoal to echinacea and turmeric.

We loved you hard and willed you to live. Magically you and all but one of your littermates survived.

Leaving our lives in California behind, we were unsure of what was next and questioned whether we could bring you along for the ride. In anguish, I asked the universe for a sign.

The very next day our ginger cat, Moxy, left us a very sweet present of mouse parts beautifully laid out on a rock in the creek bed beside the house (as he often did). But this time, beneath this lovely gift were three very shiny red sparkles. I looked closer and realized they were gems of some sort embedded in this rock.

I picked the rock up, cleaned it off, Samuel smashed it with a hammer and three spherical gems of varying sizes popped out perfectly. I held them in my hands and felt grounded, calm and at peace. These beautiful red gemstones (which we later learned were garnets) looked just like the red glowing moon on the Tarot card I had pulled the night before. I had asked it the question of whether or not we should keep you. In front of the moon was a gorgeous woman and beside her was a wolf, the only one in that deck of cards. The card read "I unleash my wild and choose to be free."

We named you Malusi, isiXhosa for shepherd and together we adventured from California to Baja on dusty desert roads in our 1980 Cheverolet truck. After Baja, you guided us home to South Africa a year before the pandemic hit. We were exactly where we needed to be because of you.

I was always afraid of death. A bolt of lightning had killed my first love; electricity plunged straight through his chest while he was working on a farm in Canada. It rocked my world. I was wrecked and the pain of living almost felt too much to bear. I had loved him from the first moment I saw him, and we had dated for around three years throughout university; and suddenly he was gone.

East Cape, Baja California Sur, shot on a Sony a6500 with a Mitakon Zhongyi fixed 35mm lens

Todos Santos, Baja California Sur, Mexico, shot on a Sony a6500 with a Mitakon Zhongyi fixed 35mm lens

Grief sends you on journeys you never thought you'd take. I wanted to numb the pain and I tried to in many different ways. After drowning my sorrows in alcohol, dabbling in drugs and partying so hard I didn't even know my own name, I found yoga and returned to my meditation in the form of cooking.

Cooking had always been a source of relaxation and a great comfort to me, and through it, unconsciously, unintentionally, I embarked on an adventure to heal my soul. I travelled through Europe: France, Belgium, Spain, and ended up living in London for four wonderful months, which still feels more like a year in my memory. It was in England that I met my soulmate, who made me believe in love again, wrote me love songs and sang them to me under our apple tree on the porch of our duplex house in Queen's Park, London.

We met on the hottest day of the year when everyone flocked to the sea at Brighton, and it was as if the universe had conspired to bring us together. From the very first moment I saw him, tunnel vision, no words, just a great knowing that he would be a massive part of my life.

We spoke for hours, and then, at four o'clock in the morning, we parted ways without exchanging numbers or even knowing each other's full name. (Later, I found his name on the wall of the backpacker hotel where we were staying). I watched him walk away that morning, up the cobbled streets toward the train station, and I wanted to shout "Come back!", but nothing came out, and I felt like I had just let something potentially life-changing walk away from me.

Monday morning came and I was staring at my computer screen, dreaming of this man, who was also called Sam. And I decided to email him. My heart was pounding, fearing rejection or no reply. In hindsight, this was one of those defining moments in my life.

"It was so lovely to meet you," I typed, "If you're ever in London, let me know." I breathed a sigh; at least I put myself out there and I wouldn't regret not reaching out.

Two minutes later an email popped up: "This morning I woke up to dirty dishes, the strongest anxiety, and a new sense of excitement. I know it sounds really cheesy because I have only met you once, but I have never felt like this before and I can't stop thinking about you.

You see the beauty in everything, you're a beautiful person, Sam, and I hope we meet again."

The words tingled through my body. So honest, real and open.

A couple of days later, there he was – Samuel Alex Miller. He surprised me at my door in London, with a guitar on his back and a joint beautifully rolled in watermelon paper in his top pocket. We were both so completely overwhelmed by the energy between us that we could hardly speak during our first moments together.

We travelled the world together on and off for the next ten years.

My travels initially began directly after university with Thailand, which completely blew me away and introduced me to real Thai food – which still remains one of my favourite cuisines of all time. I remember sitting at a street food stall in Bangkok (with all the crazy smells), experiencing the buzzing energy, eating the most memorable bowl of steaming-hot tom yum soup and nearly crying with joy at how delicious (and cheap) it was. That's the thing about Thai food: whether it's a five-star restaurant or a street food stall, it's usually equally mind-blowing in flavour and depth.

I taught English for a while in Hong Kong before I realized I was too immature to mould young minds and ran away from the "Big City Life" to a job as a photographer on a cruise liner in the Mediterranean. More magical food inspiration filtered into my life, from beautiful markets in Sardinia to steaming hot mussels served with crusty bread, thin French fries and a glass of crisp white wine at a quaint seaside restaurant in Villefranche; paella on the streets of Barcelona; rich and creamy truffle pasta in Palma de Mallorca; and the most perfect pizza in Rome.

Other highlights include a magical and life-changing three-month trip through India (which I touch on a lot in my memoirs throughout this journal), four months spent in Central America, living in Sri Lanka for five months and Baja, Mexico, for almost a year.

Living and working in California for four years was instrumental in connecting me with growing my own food and medicine – planting, harvesting, working with my hands in the earth and reconnecting to this simple yet powerful act.

What an incredible journey it has been, with the places I have lived and the people I have met all moulding my culinary story: the old lady in Sri Lanka who taught me how to make fresh coconut milk, spicy dhal on the fire, coconut sambals and other classic veggie dishes like spicy green beans and tomato, pumpkin coconut curry and mind-blowing jackfruit curry; the wonderful woman in India who showed me how to make homemade palak paneer and steaming-hot bowls of Tibetan noodle soup; the man who lived in the jungle in Thailand who taught me how to cook a traditional green Thai curry; and the wonderful soul who shared with me her mother's recipe for mushroom masala and naan breads in Goa.

I travel for food. It is through food that we gain so much joy and pleasure, and exploring a country's cuisine really gets to the heart and soul of the place.

Even if you can't speak the language, you can watch the cooking process, share a meal and enjoy being in one another's company over this universal act that brings so much fulfilment.

***

Before I left London on my travels, I awoke one night to excruciating pain searing like a blade through my right rib and back toward my shoulder blade. It felt like I was going to die. Eight gruelling hours, three hot baths and many hot water bottles later, the pain subsided and I was left bewildered. And so began my seven-year journey of trying to find out what was happening in my body and causing this pain.

It would come around every one to three months and took over in ways I cannot explain. I initially thought the pain was being caused by gallbladder attacks or gallstones. What I gradually discovered is that I felt worse when I ate animal products – and this led me into the world of plant-based eating. I was finally diagnosed with recurring kidney stones in both my kidneys. The biggest no-nos for kidney stones are alcohol, coffee, excess animal products and allergens like bleached white flour, sugar and salt. My longest pain-free period was in Sri Lanka. I replaced my morning coffee with celery juice, alcohol with smoothies, juices, kombucha and botanical drinks, and I ate no dairy, eggs or gluten.

I surfed and did yoga every day and started to connect with my body more and listen to her whispers.

My journey with yoga and my health prompted me to start eating more plant-based food, and before I had even realized it, I was choosing to eat that way most of the time. There is no doubt that a plant-based lifestyle makes me feel incredible. I have more energy, I feel lighter, my yoga practice has deepened, and so has my connection to nature and the food I am putting into my body. Suddenly, a whole new world opened up for me to explore and I began opting for food that is high vibrational, medicinal, whole and organic, and is preferably grown by myself or someone I know and trust. It is truly amazing how much food you can grow with just a little bit of land and innovative methods. There are some amazing vertical garden setups you can buy for apartments, and microgreens, which provide a lot more bioavailable nutrients than larger greens, can be grown in a really small space.

This change took my creativity in the kitchen to a completely new level as I started to explore plant-based versions of all the delicious food I had eaten on my travels. I began to appreciate seasonal ingredients, celebrating vegetables and herbs, their beautiful varieties, colours and shapes, and exploring heirloom seeds, magical rainbow carrots and beetroots/beets, gorgeous bright purple and yellow cauliflowers, pink radishes, pink, purple and red potatoes and tomatoes of all colours and sizes.

Eating the rainbow is something I try to do every day, and when I don't, I really feel the difference. Incorporating a variety of colourful vegetables and fruits into your diet encourages a diversity of healthy bacteria in your gut and provides a plethora of antioxidants, vitamins and minerals with each meal.

The recipes in this book were created as I embarked on my own healing journey, recreating plant-based alternatives to dishes I grew up eating or fell in love with on my travels. None of the recipes in this book should be taken as an attempt to recreate traditions of which I am not a part – rather, they are the result of a fusion of flavours and inspiration from my personal experiences. Food is medicine and I have included information about the healing benefits of ingredients to encourage you to connect with your food in a new way and to foster a deeper understanding of the medicinal properties of food.

Plants are so versatile and while the recipes in this book are all plant-based, they can be enjoyed by everyone. My intention is to encourage you to incorporate a variety of colourful, healing vegetables into your diet and to obtain the highest nutritional benefit possible from your meals.

There is a common misconception that eating healthily has to be time consuming and expensive, but this is not the case, and the recipes in this book are testament to that with so many of them taking under 30 minutes to cook. I have created intuitive recipes that are mostly simple, easy to follow, quick to make and highly nutritious. I have also explored some lesser-known ingredients that add an abundance of colour and nutrition to your plate.

The recipes are flexible and include ingredient alternatives to encourage you to use what you have on hand. I have never been a recipe follower; I use them for inspiration and then add my own flair and I want to encourage you to do the same with these recipes - see them as a gentle guide and then explore your own intuition and creativity in the kitchen or adapt them to fit the season and produce available to you.

I hope you find healing, comfort and love in these pages. All the blessings to you on your journey.

Karoo, South Africa, shot on a Panasonic a6500 with a Mitakon Zhongyi fixed 35mm lens

Leh, Ladakh, India, shot on a Panasonic GH4 with a fixed 50mm lens

Leh, Ladakh, India

Cooking as Meditation

The one ingredient that remains constant in all these recipes is, simply, love.

I have spent a long time trying to figure out which form of meditation works best for me, and as I studied different types (through yoga and books), I became aware of the fact that sitting cross-legged like Buddha under a tree, waiting for enlightenment, is not the only way to enter a state of meditation.

For me, personally, meditation revealed itself in the form of gardening, surfing, dancing, watching the moon rise, listening to the sound of the rain or ocean, being totally absorbed in the dancing flames of a fire or the starry night sky, and cooking and preparing food with love.

I truly believe that it boils down to a few simple things.

Vibration – our energy body and the energetic aura that expands 1.5m (5 feet) outward from our sides and 1m (3 feet) above our heads and below our feet holds specific frequencies. We also have energetic meridians that become blocked from trauma, toxins, emotions and electromagnetic frequencies. The foods we consume hold vibrational frequencies and there are certain foods that lower the vibrational energy of your body just by holding them in your hands. Nevertheless, there are high-vibrational foods such as organic fruit and vegetables that raise the vibrational energy of your body.

My meditation always starts by consciously choosing the ingredients I need to create my meals, making sure they are all organically grown and free of chemicals and pesticides, as well as seasonal.

The entire process is sacred and begs to be savoured, respected and, where possible, shared. Essentially, the love and effort you put into food is energetically assimilated into the meal and then becomes part of the mind, body and soul of the people eating it.

Cooking with passion and purpose, and knowing that your thoughts and energy will positively or negatively affect the way your food tastes, creates simple awareness in this beautiful act.

The more love and care you put in, the more magical and delicious your food will taste and the healthier it will ultimately be for you.

The Great Wall of China, shot on a Nikon D90 with a canon fixed 50mm lens

JOURNAL ENTRY //

... upon you I finally

walked ... and it was

beautiful.

There's something majestic

about a structure that took

so many years and lives to

build.

Stretching as far as the

eye can see, one can only

imagine the countless

centuries of feet that have

walked upon this vast wall.

Fall in Love with Food

Modern life has meant that we have lost our connection with the food we eat.

How many of us grow our own produce? Make our own bread? Work with our hands in the soil to grow the food we consume?

This disconnection is exacerbated by instant meals, pre-made food, takeout, vegetables chopped and sold in plastic packets, and – even more disturbing – perfectly cut, boneless meat wrapped up and ready to go.

How many of us would eat meat if we were required to kill the animal ourselves? To wring its neck or slit its throat? I don't think I could, but I do catch fish and eat them. I have done since I was a little girl and I feel no shame or sorrow in doing so. Is this wrong? No, I don't think so, and if the world still lived idyllic hunter-gatherer existences, we would not be required to take such drastic measures to right our ineffable wrongs.

Factory farming is the third largest cause of global warming that exists today. The sheer number of cows, literally being "grown" for food, produce exceptional amounts of methane which makes the atmosphere hotter.

Thirty percent of the world's ice-free surface is used not to grow food for human beings, but to support the chickens, pigs and cattle that we eat.

The toxic waste from factory farms runs into rivers and streams, polluting our water supply. And then there is the question of karma that constantly plays on my mind. This excerpt from *The Higher Taste* by A C Bhaktivedanta Swami Prabhupada sums it up perfectly:

Although we seemingly attach great value to life, each year in the world billions of defenceless animals are butchered. This wholesome slaughter of animals is not necessary to prevent us from starving. Moreover, it is economically extravagant, environmentally damaging, and ethically reprehensible. More seriously, however, animal killing violates the universal law of action and reaction.

Scientists clearly understand how the physical law of action and reaction ("for every action there is an equal and opposite reaction") applies to material objects, but most are unaware of the more subtle laws of action and reaction in the realm of consciousness.

I am not here to preach about being a perfect vegan. I still eat seafood, cheese and butter from

the dairy down the road and some pasture-raised chicken or beef or wild venison like kudu when I feel like my body needs it.

I want to share with you that eating plant-based whole foods is something you can incorporate into your life bit by bit. Maybe one meal a day to start, then one day a week, then a couple of days a week, until you find the balance that works for you.

Our ancestors hunted for hours, sometimes days on end, to find their food which they feasted on with their entire tribe and then dried and preserved to last them as long as possible. Our current appetite for meat in all forms is insatiable, unnatural and causes a major imbalance on the planet.

If we all ate more whole foods and plants, our individual health and the health of the planet would improve dramatically. As consumers we have the power to drive change by supporting local farmers, becoming aware of how our food is grown and produced, and making healthy choices that are also kind to the planet.

May cooking no longer be a chore, but something you savour and relish, a chance to create magic. Allow cooking to fuel your creativity, release your tension and become a form of meditation. Every meal is medicine and serves as a way to nourish and heal your mind, body and soul.

I don't always use standard measurements like cups and grams and prefer to describe ingredients by touch and feel – in handfuls, pinches and sprinkles. Every sense is involved in this process, and this (re)connection with our food fosters a healthy relationship with it and its journey from the ground to the plate. From foraging and gathering to growing and picking fruits and vegetables, our connection to what we eat has been severed – and the general health of our populations indicates that we desperately need to find ways to repair it.

So, dim the lights, light some candles, pour yourself a glass of wine or roll a joint and turn the music up … It's time to nourish your mind, body and soul with simple, seasonal, high-vibrational plant-based recipes that won't break the bank. They are delicious, nutritious and flavourful alternatives to your meat-based favourites as well as new creations that will blow your mind.

I have included memoirs from my travels, little snippets of a place from where a recipe comes, and moments along the road of which the smell or taste of a dish still reminds me.

Whether you are opening up to the idea of plant-based eating

for the first time or you want to incorporate more plant-based cooking into your life, this journal has something for everyone.

I always pretended I was on a cooking show when I started spending time in the kitchen at about the age of ten. When most children were watching cartoons, I was binging on cooking programmes, and I often used whatever was in the fridge or pantry to create something like they did on *Ready, Steady, Cook*.

Growing up in South Africa, my family would always have people around on the weekends, cooking wonderful things together outside on the fire, dancing, sharing good food and drinking. We went musselling and oyster foraging and my parents taught us how to get bait and catch fish, fostering a love of nature and the outdoors. Mum's mussel soup is one of my fondest food memories, always cooked in a black cast iron pot on the fire with lots of onion, garlic, white wine and the freshest mussels we had foraged that morning.

With Dad we'd make oxtail potjie and lamb stews, always outside on the fire. Every Sunday, we'd get excited about what we were going to cook that day.

I was fortunate to also have an African Mother who taught me lessons in the kitchen. She has this grounding mother earth energy and laughs from her belly. Her food is warm and nourishing and full of

My intention with this journal is to gently guide and inspire anyone who is interested in the magic of plant-based food.

love – from cottage pies to a classic macaroni and cheese and the traditional, nostalgically comforting isiXhosa dish umngqusho (a samp and beans concoction smothered in butter and salt).

Growing up in South Africa meant we ate meat two to three times a day. It was the focal point of the meal: first, it was decided what meat you would have, then how you would prepare it and finally what veggies you would serve it with.

I began feeling sick after eating rich meats such as pork. I loved all meats and never refused a lamb shank or crispy pork belly. My body decided for me by feeling nauseous every time I ate certain fatty meats. Because my nature is to learn and research, I devoured anything I could find about our food and our body, and I have become very committed to opting for pasture-raised, organic, local and whole foods where possible.

This journey has brought me to where I am now and given me a greater understanding of conscious eating. To be able to eat intuitively, with gratitude by listening to our bodies, is one of the greatest gifts we can give ourselves.

Calaveras, California, United States, shot on a Pentax K1000 with a fixed 35 mm lens

Adaptogens

(in herbal medicine) a natural substance considered to help the body adapt to stress and to exert a normalizing effect upon bodily processes.

Adaptogens are said to increase physical performance and reduce mental fatigue and the physical effects of stress on the body.

I use my adaptogens in smoothies, mainly. A combination of maca, moringa, ashwagandha and mushrooms with cacao in a smoothie is delicious. They're also great added to raw deserts and chocolate, juices and soups or taken in veggie capsules daily.

Ashwagandha (or Indian ginseng) is said to stabilize cortisol levels. It is both energizing and calming, and it enhances memory and cognition.

Mucuna pruriens (a tropical legume native to Africa) contains high levels of naturally occurring L-dopa, which is the precursor to dopamine. Dopamine is an important neurotransmitter that is essential for sleep, memory, mood, mental functions, and calming the nervous system.

Maca was revered in ancient Inca culture as a hormone balancer, increasing strength, the immune system and libido, particularly in women.

Moringa is an antioxidant and anti-inflammatory that balances hormones, slows the effects of aging, improves digestive health, protects and nourishes the skin and helps with balancing blood sugar levels.

Reishi mushroom is revered for longevity. It supports healthy cholesterol levels and prevents plaque formation, improves immune function, and promotes healthy liver and kidneys.

Chaga mushroom stimulates the immune system, is a potent anti-viral and reduces inflammation.

Holy basil is antimicrobial, anti-diabetic and anti-inflammatory. It's helpful for the circulatory, immune and nervous systems.

Healing herbs and spices

basil
black pepper
cacao
cannabis
cardamom
cayenne pepper
chlorella
cinnamon
cloves
cordyceps
coriander/cilantro
cumin
fennel
ginger
lemongrass
lion's mane
mint
mustard seeds
oregano
parsley
peppermint
rosemary
sage
shiitake
spirulina
thyme
turmeric

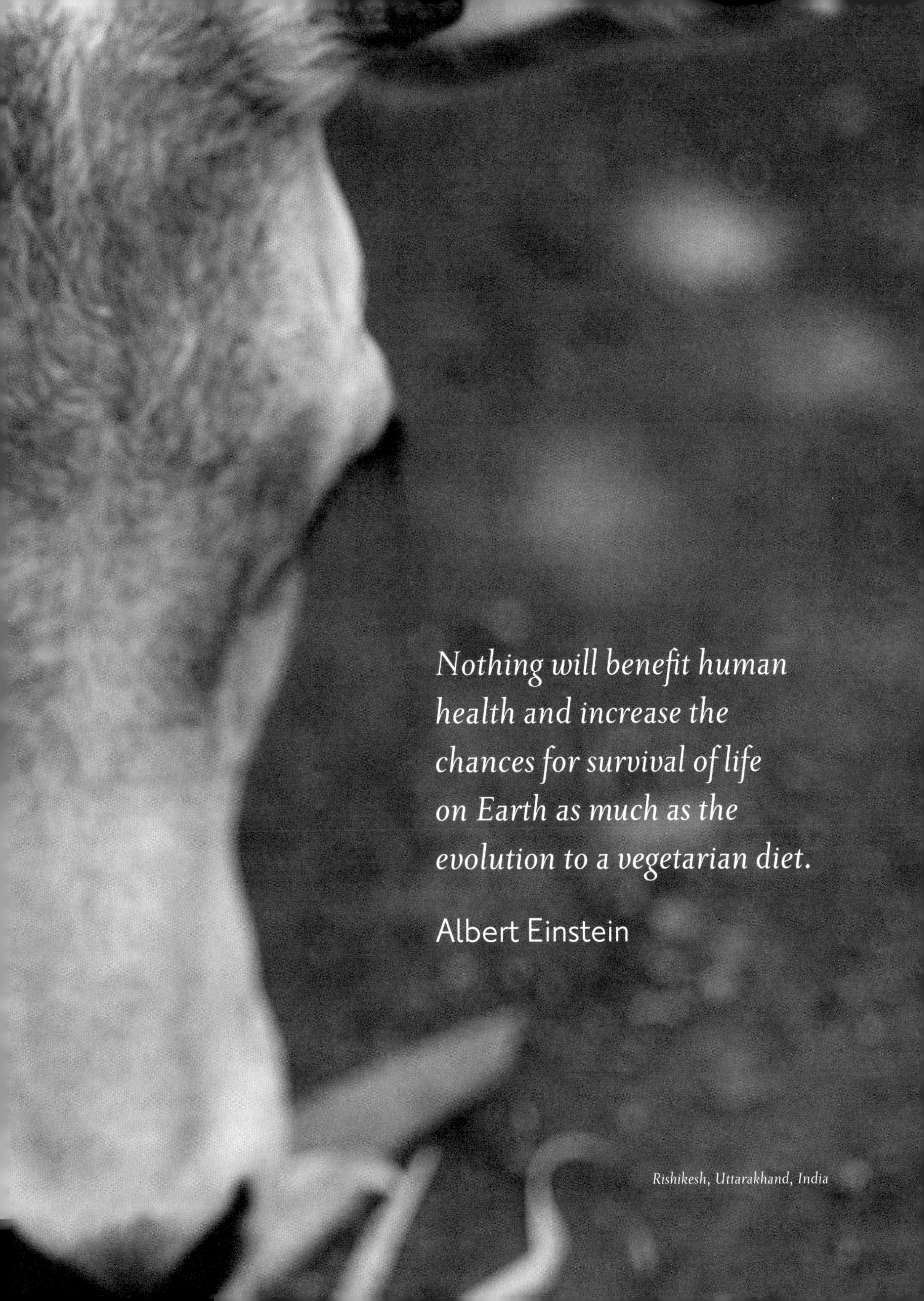

Nothing will benefit human health and increase the chances for survival of life on Earth as much as the evolution to a vegetarian diet.

Albert Einstein

Rishikesh, Uttarakhand, India

Water the Healer

I have always found myself drawn to living near water. From the ocean, to rivers, waterfalls and lakes – I feel calmed and peaceful in the presence of this powerful element.

In Masaru Emoto's book *The True Power of Water*, he says:

We must pay respect to water, feel love and gratitude, and receive vibrations with a positive attitude. Then, water changes, you change, and I change. Because both you and I are water.

A recent study showed that London is drinking the Thames, that the water pouring out of the taps has a number of chemicals such as chlorine added to it for purification purposes, which is unfortunately the case in most cities worldwide. Tap water may also contain fluoride, heavy metals (such as lead and mercury), pesticides and pharmaceutical residues. These substances, although in trace amounts, can have cumulative effects on our health over time.

Chlorine may contribute to respiratory issues and skin irritation, fluoride may lead to dental and skeletal fluorosis, heavy metals have been linked to organ damage and developmental issues and pesticides and pharmaceuticals may disrupt hormonal balance and pose long-term health risks.

The truth is that all water on earth is now tainted. At Mount Shasta, in Northern California, tests revealed extremely high levels of barium and other metals in the water. This is believed to be some of the purest water in America, but a very limited amount of such water exists, what with a massive increase in toxic metals and chemicals being sprayed into the skies for weather modification programmes, as well as increased amounts of agricultural toxic waste, runoff and microplastics.

Most of the water we currently drink is essentially dead and lifeless. Water was intended to be consumed directly from a flowing stream, alive and charged. Unless your water comes from a spring, a river or a water ionizing machine, you are receiving absolutely no nutritional benefits from the water you drink. Even water sitting in a rainwater tank is dead, as it is stagnant and has been for some time.

If you don't have access to a flowing water spring or very fresh rainwater, there are some effective options available: high-quality water filtration systems can remove contaminants; boiling water may eliminate certain microbes, but not all chemicals; distillation condenses the steam from water, leaving contaminants behind; activated carbon filters are effective at removing chlorine and some organic contaminants; and water-ionizing machines, although expensive, make use of filters which remove all contaminants and then ionize and charge the water so it is more effectively absorbed by the body.

JOURNAL ENTRY //

This river is the magical Río Celeste ~ Costa
Rica … the place where two rivers meet …

The sky-blue colour of the Rio Celeste is
produced by the dispersion of light by colloidal
aluminoscilicate particles.

It is said that when the creator was painting
the sky blue, she dipped her brush in this river
leaving it milky turquoise forever.

Rio Celeste, Guanacaste, Costa Rica, shot on Pentax K1000 with fixed 35mm lens

Intermittent Fasting

Is breakfast really the most important meal of the day? If you look at the word break-(the)-fast, it pretty much describes exactly what is happening. A meal that breaks your fast from the night before.

If my last meal was at 7pm, I try not to eat before 11am the next day. If I eat my last meal by 5pm, then I eat breakfast around 9am the following day.

Giving your body a 16-hour gap between dinner and your first meal the next day allows you to fast every day, which helps to regulate blood sugar, slow down the aging process and maintain a natural, healthy weight.

For women, I recommend only fasting in this way during your ovulatory and follicular phases of your cycle. During pre-menstrual and menstrual phases, aim for a 12-hour fasting window and stick to having breakfast within 1–2 hours of waking up. As women we require different nutritional needs at the different stages of our cycle

and therefore should not try to fast consistently throughout the month, which is effective for men.

When you give your cells a rest from having to constantly digest food, you aid the regeneration of new, healthy and stronger cells and encourage the death of weaker, diseased cells. That hungry feeling in your tummy before you eat? Savour it and reframe it as all your cells regenerating before you break your fast.

I also try to fast one day a week where I refrain from eating solid foods and, depending on how I am feeling, either do a straight water, herbal tea or raw, organic cold-pressed juice cleanse. This works well on a Monday, to reset your body and mind for the week and bring intention to your health and food choices.

The beauty is that it does not have to be regimented and once you begin to listen to your body you will crave certain things at certain times and be able to respond accordingly.

Fasting is a way to regularly come into alignment with your higher self by being more aware, in tune and at one with your body. Intermittent fasting, along with a whole-foods, plant-based diet with some high-quality eggs, dairy, meat and fish, meditation and exercise, supplemented with medicinal spices and adaptogens, really makes the most sense to me.

Intermittent fasting has been shown to promote insulin sensitivity, suppress inflammation and reduce oxidative damage, as well as improve immune function, lower blood pressure, reduce risk of heart disease, increase longevity, improve cognitive function and protect against neurological diseases such as dementia, Alzheimers and Parkinsons. As you can see, it has a lot of benefits!

I also try to do a longer detox/ fast/cleanse twice a year for optimum healing benefits. Fasting may not be for everyone, but I encourage you to give it a try.

Pantry Staples

Oils
avocado oil
coconut oil
olive oil
sesame oil
sunflower oil

Grains
barley
buckwheat
brown/black/red/wild rice
oats
quinoa
spelt

Dried Pulses
chickpeas/garbanzo beans
brown lentils
red lentils
yellow lentils
black beans
white beans

Jars/Cans
chickpeas/garbanzo beans
coconut milk
kidney beans
black beans
butter beans
tomatoes

Sauces
apple cider vinegar
balsamic vinegar
coconut aminos
red wine vinegar
tamari/soy sauce (liquid aminos
are a good gluten-free alternative)

Adaptogens
ashwagandha
cacao
goji berries
hemp powder/seeds
maca
medicinal mushrooms
moringa

Spices
black pepper
cardamom pods
chilli flakes
cinnamon sticks
coriander
cumin
mustard seeds
nutritional yeast
paprika
red chilli powder
turmeric
white pepper

Sweeteners
agave
coconut sugar
maple syrup

Nuts, Seeds & Butters
almond butter
almonds
cacao butter
cashews
chia
coconut
coconut butter
flax
peanut butter
peanuts
pumpkin
sesame
sunflower
walnuts

Flours
almond flour
buckwheat flour
chickpea flour
coconut flour
oat flour
spelt flour
stoneground rye flour

Lingo

Blitz: To blend at a high speed.

Delish: A short version of the word delicious.

Drizzle: More than a splash and less than a glug.

Dukkah: An Egyptian and Middle Eastern crunchy topping of herbs, toasted nuts, sesame seeds and spices.

Glug: About 2 tablespoons. That is, the amount required to coat a pan, or until the bottle audibly "glugs".

Handful: A hand full of ingredients.

Lashings: Spoonfuls lathered over a dish.

Moreish: An informal word used to describe a food or drink that makes you want to have more of it.

Parm: A short version of the word Parmesan.

Pulse: To briefly start and stop a food processor in order to chop, but leave ingredients chunky.

Sarmie: Slang for the word sandwich.

Sprinkle: To distribute or disperse something randomly or irregularly throughout or on top of the dish.

Toast: To dry-fry seeds, nuts or spices in a pan on the stove until golden brown.

Cookware

I can't stress enough the importance of the pots and pans you use in your everyday cooking. For a long time we have been sold a lie: that non-stick cookware is safe. However, there are many studies that show the dangers of cooking your food in chemically coated pots and pans.

There are so many good alternatives such as glass, cast iron, china and clay. They may be pricier, but they last forever if you take good care of them.

For cast iron pans, never use soap; always clean with hot water and then use a cloth to coat the pan with vegetable oil to prevent rusting.

Purple cabbage, beetroot and green chilli sauce

The Art of Fermentation

One of the best things you can do for your gut is to add fermented foods to your diet on a daily basis.

Probiotics are live bacteria and yeasts that balance the pH of your gut and increase the general health of your digestive system by eliminating toxins and harmful bacteria.

Just one tablespoon of fermented food per meal helps with digestion, gas, bloating and overall gut health.

See page 36–7 for a great Sunshine Sauerkraut recipe with fermented cabbage. You can also try this method with any of your favourite vegetables. I love using red cabbage, beetroot/beets, carrots, kale, cucumbers and combinations of veggies with added ginger or turmeric, coriander seeds and other herbs.

When fermenting vegetables other than cabbage, it is not neccessary to massage them like we do in the recipe on page 36–7 – simply cover them in brine in a jar, place the lid on and let it do it's thing. A salt brine with a ratio of 2:3 salt to water is generally a good starting point for fermenting many different vegetables. This concentration prevents the growth of undesirable bacteria while encouraging the growth of beneficial lactic acid bacteria.

2 per cent brine: This is suitable for most vegetables, such as cucumbers, carrots, peppers and beans. It provides a good balance between preserving the vegetables and allowing fermentation to take place at a moderate pace.

3 per cent brine: This stronger brine is ideal for fermenting tougher or denser vegetables like cabbage (for sauerkraut), beetroot/beets and turnips. It helps to ensure a longer shelf life and firmer texture.

Calculating brine: To make a 2 per cent brine, use 20g/¾oz of salt per 1 litre/24fl oz/4¼ cups of water. For a 3 per cent brine, use 30g/1oz of salt per 1 litre/24fl oz/4¼ cups of water.

Check your ferment daily for the first few days. Bubbles, a tangy smell and a slight change in color are normal signs of fermentation.

Sunshine Sauerkraut

with turmeric and black pepper

makes 1 x 750ml jar
fermenting time: 3 days to 1 month

YOU WILL NEED

1 medium cabbage (i)
salt
2 tsp ground turmeric
2 tsp black pepper

METHOD

1 Grate or shred the cabbage. Save a large cabbage leaf to place over the top of the sauerkraut.

2 Grab your jar and sterilize it by washing it with boiling water. Keep your work surface and hands super clean to avoid contamination with unwanted bacteria.

3 In a glass bowl, sprinkle salt over the cabbage and massage it with your hands, pressing and kneading it until it begins to release liquid (around 5 minutes).

4 Leave to rest for 30 minutes or longer. The salt will draw the liquid from the cabbage. You will know it is ready once there is enough liquid to cover the cabbage. Stir in the turmeric and black pepper with a wooden spoon.

5 Transfer the cabbage to the sterilized jar. Pack it in tightly, making sure it is covered in brine before pressing down to prevent any air bubbles from forming. If you don't have enough brine, add some filtered water.

6 Place your reserved cabbage leaf over the top of the cabbage. Using the cabbage leaf as a lid, press down on the contents of the jar, making sure that everything is submerged in brine and that the leaf covers the surface area so there is no exposure to oxygen.

7 Close the lid of the jar and store in a dark place, opening it every day to release excess gas.

8 The cabbage will be lacto-fermented in about 3 days, but will continue to ferment for a stronger flavour for up to 1 month. Place it in the fridge to keep for up to 4–6 months.

Turmeric is a powerful anti-inflammatory and, when consumed with black pepper, is absorbed by the body at a much higher rate because the piperine in black pepper facilitates the absorption of the curcumin in turmeric by up to 2000%.

I ate this sunshine kraut in the magical town of Todos Santos, in Baja California Sur, Mexico, and instantly fell in love. I find the colour of food to be incredibly stimulating, and the vibrant yellow of this sauerkraut reminds me that it is medicine. I love adding a spoonful of this to pretty much every meal I eat. This is an effective way of building a balanced and resilient gut biome and aiding in the digestion of your food.

The specific salinity for sauerkraut is around 2%. In order to calculate 2% salinity: weight of your cabbage in grams x 0.2 (2%) = amount of salt in grams.

NOTE

i When portioning your salt and cabbage, the general rule to follow is about 1 tablespoon of salt per 1¾lb/800g) of cabbage.

Dressed Up

These are some of my favourite sauces, dips, spreads and crunchy toppings to dress your dishes up - simple flavour bombs that will elevate your meals. I imagine the sauces and dips like paints on an artist's palette, colourfully ripped over salads, roasted vegetables, curries and other delicious morsels, the crunchy toppings add a layer of texture and ferments provide your daily dose of probiotics. Many of these recipes require a blender, food processor or pestle and mortar.

Crunchy Toppings

I am obsessed with crunchy toppings on just about anything, from salads to soups and curries. Texture is so important for me in a meal, and a crunchy topping really adds another dimension to the experience, taking the meal to a whole new level in such a simple way.

DUKKAH

For a delicious snack, dip crusty bread first into olive oil and then into this dukkah.

75g/2⅔oz/⅔ cup nuts (hazelnuts/
    almonds/walnuts)
80g/2¾oz/½ cup sesame seeds
2 tbsp cumin seeds
2 tbsp coriander seeds
salt and pepper

Preheat the oven to 180°C/350°F/Gas 4. Spread the nuts out on a baking sheet and toast for 5 minutes in the oven until golden. Place in a tea towel and rub vigorously to remove the skins.
Toast the sesame seeds in a pan on a medium heat for 3–5 minutes until golden, then pour into a food processor.
In the same pan, toast the cumin and coriander seeds for 1–2 minutes until fragrant, then transfer to the food processor and pulse until fine. Add the nuts and seeds and pulse together with the spices, salt and pepper until just combined and the mixture is somewhat chunky. Use on salads, veg, soups, stews and dips.

SMOKY COCONUT BACON

When fried in coconut oil and salt, the coconut turns into a golden, crunchy, smoky, salty bacon-like topping.

1 tbsp coconut oil
pinch of salt
pinch of paprika
pinch of pepper
2 handfuls of dried coconut
    flakes or fresh brown
    coconut, thinly sliced

Heat the coconut oil in a pan on a medium heat, then add the salt and spices and fry for 30 seconds until melted and fragrant. Add the coconut and cook until golden brown and crispy, about 2 minutes. Pat with a paper towel before sprinkling over pastas, soups, salads and curries.

FRIED NUT AND SEED MIX

a few glugs of olive oil
70g/2⅓oz/½ cup pumpkin seeds
70gg/2⅓oz/½ cup nuts, roughly
    chopped (your choice)
80g/2⅔oz/½ cup sesame seeds
75g/2⅔oz/½ cup sunflower seeds
2 tbsp nutritional yeast
1 tbsp dried oregano
1 tbsp dried thyme
2 garlic cloves, diced
salt and pepper, to taste
squeeze of lemon juice

Heat the oil in a frying pan over a medium heat. Add all the ingredients except the lemon juice and fry for 3–5 minutes until browned and crunchy. Remove the pan from the heat, squeeze the lemon juice over the mixture and toss to coat evenly. Spread out on a baking tray to cool and dry. Serve on salads, veggies, soups, curries and stews.

Smoky coconut bacon

PEANUT, LIME & CHILLI

75g/2⅔oz/½ cup peanuts
zest and juice of 2 lemons or limes
1–2 green chillies
salt and pepper

Pulse the peanuts, zest and chillies
in a food processor until fine.
Stir in the lemon juice, salt
and pepper to taste.
Use on top of stir fries, Asian-
inspired dishes, soups and curries.

COCONUT SAMBAL

One of my favourites toppings
from Sri Lanka. Ideally use
fresh brown coconuts, but dried
shredded coconut also works,
as does grated or desiccated.

80g/2¾oz/1 cup desiccated/
   shredded coconut,
   dried or fresh
80g/2¾oz/1 cup coconut flakes
2 tsp chilli powder
4 garlic cloves, crushed
zest and juice of 1 lemon/lime
salt and pepper

Combine all the ingredients in
a bowl until evenly mixed.
Serve with your favourite curry,
or on top of soups or stews.

SPICY INDIAN ALMONDS

2 tbsp coconut oil/ghee/butter
thumb-sized piece of
   root ginger, sliced
2 tbsp cumin seeds
2 red chillies, halved
2 bay leaves
2 handfuls of flaked/
   sliced almonds
4 garlic cloves, sliced
salt and pepper

Melt the coconut oil in a frying pan,
add the ginger, cumin, chillies and
bay leaves and fry for 30 seconds.
Add the almonds and garlic and
fry for 2–5 minutes until golden.
Stir frequently or shake the pan to
ensure even cooking and prevent
burning. Serve over curries,
soups, roasted veggies and salads.

ROASTED CAULIFLOWER TOPPING

½ head cauliflower, broken
   into florets
1 tsp cumin
1 tsp paprika
1 tsp turmeric
handful of sunflower seeds
1 tbsp olive oil
salt and pepper

Preheat the oven to
180°C/350°F/Gas 4.
In a bowl, mix the ingredients
together until well coated. Spread
the mixture out in a roasting pan
and roast until golden, around
20 minutes. Pulse in a food
processor until coarse crumbs
form. Serve sprinkled over salads,
soups, vegetables and curries.

SAVOURY GRANOLA

175g/6oz/2 cups rolled oats
90g/3¼oz/½ cup
  buckwheat groats
70g/2½oz/½ cup pumpkin seeds
70g/2¾oz/½ cup sunflower seeds
60g/2¼oz/½ cup hazelnuts

FOR THE DRESSING

75ml/2⅔fl oz/½ cup olive oil
2 tbsp dried oregano
2 tbsp rosemary
2 tbsp thyme
1 tbsp honey
zest of 1 orange/lemon
salt and pepper

*Preheat the oven to
160°C/320°F/Gas 3.
Combine all the dressing
ingredients in a large bowl
and whisk until smooth.
Add all the dry ingredients
to the bowl, then use your
hands or a spatula to toss in
the dressing until coated.
Roast in the oven until golden
brown, around 20 minutes. Around
the halfway mark (10 minutes),
toss the ingredients on the tray to
prevent them from becoming soggy.*

SOURDOUGH CRUNCH

*This is a good way to use
day-old bread that's a little
stale and less delish*

couple of slices of sourdough,
  cut into bite-size pieces
olive oil
1 tsp dried oregano
1 tsp chilli flakes
1 tsp garlic powder
salt and pepper

*Preheat the oven to
180°C/350°F/Gas 4.
Spread the bread out on a baking
sheet, drizzle with olive oil,
sprinkle with the spices, salt
and pepper and bake for about
15 minutes until crunchy.*

VEGAN PARM

150g/5¼oz/1 cup sunflower
  seeds, toasted
2 tbsp nutritional yeast
1 garlic clove
1 tsp dried oregano
salt and pepper

*Put all the ingredients into a
food processor and pulse 2–3
times so that the seeds remain
slightly chunky. Sprinkle on
pasta, pizza, veg and salads.*

MEDITERRANEAN DREAM

handful of pitted olives, torn
1–2 chillies, diced
thumb-sized piece of
  root ginger, diced
zest and juice of 1 lemon
2 tbsp coriander seeds, toasted
  and roughly chopped
handful of nuts (any kind),
  toasted and roughly chopped
handful of fresh coriander/
  cilantro, roughly chopped

*Combine all the ingredients
in a bowl until evenly mixed.
Sprinkle this over curries, soups,
roasted vegetables and salads.*

ASIAN CRUNCH

80g/2¾oz/½ cup sesame seeds
10g/⅓oz/½ cup nori
  (seaweed) flakes
15g/½oz/½ cup crispy onions
2 tbsp red chilli flakes

*Toast the sesame seeds in a dry pan
on a medium heat for 3–5 minutes
until golden, then pour into a bowl.
Combine with all the remaining
ingredients and use as a topping on
stir-fries, soups, veggies and salads*

42

Tzatziki

YOU WILL NEED

½ cucumber, peeled
1 garlic clove, crushed
1 tbsp lemon juice
8 tbsp coconut or plain yoghurt
⅓ tsp ground cumin
glug of olive oil
salt and white pepper, to taste
small handful of fresh mint or dill, to serve

METHOD

1   Halve the cucumber lengthways and
    scrape the seeds out using a teaspoon.
    Grate the cucumber and squeeze out
    excess water using your hands.

2   Combine with all other ingredients
    (except the mint or dill) in a bowl.
    Top with fresh mint and/or dill and
    a drizzle of olive oil.

Toasted Coriander/ Cilantro Dressing

with spring onions/scallions, olive oil and lemon juice

YOU WILL NEED

1 tsp coriander seeds
juice of 1 lemon
1 spring onion/scallion, sliced
1 tsp agave/coconut sugar
2–4 tbsp olive oil
salt and pepper

METHOD

1   Toast the coriander seeds in a dry pan on a medium heat for 1–2 minutes until fragrant. Crush in a pestle and mortar.

2   Shake together in a jar with the rest of the ingredients.

3   Pour over your favourite salad or veggies.

Ginger & Turmeric Sauce

YOU WILL NEED

1 tsp ground turmeric

1 tsp grated root ginger

2 handfuls of sunflower seeds (i)or cashew nuts,
    soaked (ii)

juice of 1 lemon

75ml/2½fl oz/⅓ cup water

salt and black pepper

1 tbsp olive oil

METHOD

1   In a blender or food processor, blend all
    the ingredients until smooth and creamy.

NOTES

i   If using sunflower seeds, toast them dry in a pan for
     a nuttier flavour.
ii   Soak your cashew nuts in freshly boiled water for
     15–30 minutes for easier blending.

Cheesiest "No-Cheese" Sauce

I first made this vegan cheese sauce with cashew nuts, but wanted to find an alternative that was more cost-effective. Sunflower seeds, when toasted, produce a delicious nutty flavour that works so well in creamy sauces. This is a total crowd-pleaser and can be your creamy base for any flavoured sauce you wish to make. Don't get me wrong, this sauce is equally delicious made with cashew nuts - use the same quantity, but remember to soak them in boiling hot water for 15 minutes before blending.

YOU WILL NEED

palm-sized piece of yellow pepper

1 tsp nutritional yeast, optional (i)

glug of olive oil

150g/5¼oz/1 cup sunflower seeds, toasted

juice of ½ lemon

250ml/9fl oz/1 cup water

½ garlic clove, optional

½ tsp tumeric

salt and pepper

METHOD

1   Blend all the ingredients until smooth and creamy, adding more water as needed for your desired consistency.

2   Warm slightly before serving.

NOTE

i   This adds an extra cheesy element to the sauce, but it is completely optional.

Smoky Romesco Sauce

YOU WILL NEED

2 large red peppers

2 large ripe tomatoes

2 handfuls of almonds

3 tbsp olive oil

2 tsp smoked paprika

2 cloves of raw or roasted garlic (i)

squeeze of lemon juice

salt and pepper

METHOD

1　Blister the red peppers and tomatoes over an open flame or grill/broil them in the oven for 5–10 minutes until charred and blackened. Place the peppers and tomatoes in a container with a lid to steam for around 5 minutes. Remove from the container and leave to cool for 5–10 minutes, then remove their skins by running them under cold water.

2　Roast the almonds in the oven or dry-fry in a frying pan on a medium heat for about 5–7 minutes until they brown slightly to bring out their nutty flavour.

3　In a food processor or pestle and mortar, combine all the ingredients well. Traditionally, the consistency is almost like a pesto, but smooth and creamy is delicious too – play around and have fun.

NOTE

i　Roasting the garlic gives it a sweeter, less intense flavour than using it raw. Drizzle a whole head of garlic with some olive oil and sprinkle with salt. Wrap in tinfoil and roast in the oven at 180°C/350°F/Gas mark 4 for 25–30 minutes until the garlic is soft enough to squeeze out with ease.

Beetroot/Beet, Ginger & Lemon Sauce

Betalains in beetroot/beets support liver function by aiding in the detoxification process. They assist in protecting the liver from oxidative damage and the elimination of toxins from the body.

This sauce is delicious with the Herby Oat & Sweet Potato Balls on page 221, the Aubergine/Eggplant Schnitzels on page 216, the Crumbled Cauliflower Bites on page 191 and the Vietnamese Rice Paper Rolls on page 256.

YOU WILL NEED

1 small raw beetroot/beet, peeled and quartered

1 tsp grated root ginger

handful of sunflower seeds, toasted

juice of 1 lemon

75ml/2½fl oz/⅓ cup water

salt and pepper

METHOD

1   In a food processor, blend all the ingredients until smooth and creamy.

Green Olive Tapenade

with capers and garlic

A handful of olives every day provides a great source of healthy fats as well as vitamins A and E. Olives are loaded with phenolic compounds such as squalene, which is a potent antioxidant. Antioxidants are free radical scavengers, meaning they protect cells from damage.

YOU WILL NEED

380g/13⅓oz/1½ cups pitted green olives

75ml/2½fl oz/⅓ cup olive oil

juice of 1 lemon/lime

2 garlic cloves

2 tbsp capers

handful of parsley

2 tbsp grated lemon/lime zest

METHOD

1   Pulse all the ingredients in a food processor until chunky. You can also use a pestle and mortar.

2   Serve on sandwiches, crackers, veggies, burgers, with salads, or as a pasta pesto.

Basil Pesto

Basil pesto is traditionally made with pine nuts but in this recipe, I've swapped them out for toasted sunflower or pumpkin seeds. Rocket/arugula, parsley, coriander/cilantro, mint and sundried tomatoes are all delicious options for pesto.

YOU WILL NEED

2 large handfuls of fresh basil (i)

handful of sunflower/pumpkin seeds, toasted

I small garlic clove

4–6 tbsp olive oil (or more as needed)

juice of ½ lemon

salt and pepper

METHOD

1   Blanch the basil in boiling water for 5–10 seconds and then immediately transfer it to a bowl of icy water for 5 minutes to preserve its bright green colour. (ii)

2   Using a pestle and mortar or food processor, combine the basil, seeds and garlic, leaving the mixture slightly chunky.

3   Stir in the olive oil, lemon juice, salt and pepper.

NOTES

i   Rocket/arugula, parsley, coriander/cilantro or mint would work perfectly.

ii   This step is optional but does help give this pesto it's lovely bright green colour, as well as mkaing the basil leaves easier to grind

Turkish Sauce

My favourite dairy-free yoghurt is coconut. It is really tasty to cook with and makes a great savoury sauce. This sauce is traditionally served with eggs; the yoghurt base is topped with poached eggs and then lathered in the paprika garlic oil.

YOU WILL NEED

500g/1lb 1oz/2 cups yoghurt

juice and zest of 1 large lemon

salt and pepper

4 garlic cloves, sliced (i)

2 tsp paprika

4 tbsp olive oil

METHOD

1   Combine the yoghurt with the lemon juice, lemon zest, salt and pepper.

2   In a pan on a very low heat, sauté the garlic and paprika in the olive oil for 2–3 minutes until golden.

3   Pour the oil over the yoghurt, adding salt and pepper to taste.

NOTE

i   When garlic is chopped, minced or crushed, it produces allicin. This compound is responsible for many of garlic's health benefits, including its antimicrobial, anti-inflammatory, and antioxidant properties. Leave garlic to rest for 5–10 minutes before cooking to allow time for this enzymatic reaction to take place.

Green Goddess Dressing

This dressing is a firm favourite and a wonderful way of getting your daily greens and herbs in. A good trick is to blanch the herbs in boiling water for 5–10 seconds and then immediately transfer them to a bowl of icy water to preserve their bright green colour. You can store this dressing in a jar in the fridge for up to 3 days.

YOU WILL NEED

2 handfuls of fresh green herbs (i)

handful of nuts/seeds (ii)

juice of I lemon

75ml/2½fl oz/⅓ cup water

salt and pepper

2 tbsp olive oil

I garlic clove

2 large spring onions/scallions

I tsp agave (optional)

METHOD

1   In a food processor, blend all the ingredients until smooth and creamy, adding more water if needed to reach your desired consistency.

NOTES

i   You could choose from parsley, mint or coriander/cilantro. Coriander/cilantro is a powerful heavy metal detoxifier, anti-inflammatory and antioxidant.

ii   Toast seeds in a dry pan for 3–5 minutes for a nuttier flavour.

BBQ Sauce

with dates, chilli and liquid smoke

I crave the smoky, sweet and salty taste of this barbeque sauce every now and then. It perfectly caramelizes when heated and works wonderfully basted on veggies when cooking on the fire, grilling or baking. If you don't have liquid smoke, use smoked paprika for that added smoky flavour.

YOU WILL NEED

6 medjool dates, pitted

250g/9oz/1 cup tomatoes, chopped

1 red chilli

¼ tsp liquid smoke or 1 tsp smoked paprika

1 tbsp coconut sugar

1 tbsp liquid aminos/soy sauce

1 tbsp mustard

75ml/2½fl oz/⅓ cup water

METHOD

1   In a food processor, blend all the ingredients until smooth and creamy.

Ginger, Chilli & Garlic Sauce

I use this moreish mixture daily. If I'm not lathering it over hummus on rye toast, I am spooning it into my soup or onto a cracker. It is ideal to have in a jar in the fridge, as these three ingredients are the beautiful beginning of a lot of magical dishes.

YOU WILL NEED

1 palm-sized piece of root ginger

2–8 garlic cloves (i)

handful of chillies

4–6 tbsp olive oil (or more as needed)

squeeze of lemon juice

salt

METHOD

1   In a food processor, pulse the ginger, garlic and chillies until combined but still chunky.

2   Transfer to a glass jar. Cover with olive oil and add a squeeze of lemon juice and salt to taste.

NOTE

i   The amount of garlic you add is entirely up to you - raw garlic can be quite harsh so start by adding two cloves, taste, and add more as you like.

Salsa Macha

Salsa macha is a very thick and unusual salsa that comes from the state of Veracruz, located along the coast of the Gulf of Mexico. It is made by frying dried chipotle chillies (mainly the Morita kind) in a generous amount of olive oil, along with garlic cloves. Some versions add fresh chillies such as serranos or jalapeños into the mix. Peanuts and sesame seeds are added too. I didn't eat this salsa in Veracruz, but in Oaxaca and I'll never forget it. It was one of those food moments where everything danced on my tongue in perfect harmony – the spicy chillies and garlic, rich olive oil, crunchy peanuts and sesame seeds, sour vinegar and sweet sugar. It is by far my favourite chilli sauce of all time. Pure moreish bliss. If you can't find chipotle chillies, use any whole dried chillies or chilli flakes.

YOU WILL NEED

350ml/12fl oz/1½ cups olive oil

4 garlic cloves, sliced

about 120g/4¼oz/2 cups dried chipotle chillies (i), destemmed, deseeded and torn into pieces

40g/1½oz/⅓ cup unsalted peanuts

2 tbsp sesame seeds

1 tsp sea salt (or to taste)

1 tbsp coconut sugar

3 tbsp red wine vinegar

METHOD

1   Set a large heavy frying pan on a medium heat and pour in the oil. Once the oil is hot, but not smoking, add the garlic cloves. Fry for about 1 minute until they start to gain colour.

2   Add the chipotle chillies and peanuts, stir and fry for about 2 minutes. Add the sesame seeds, stir and continue to fry for about 1 minute. Remove from the heat.

3   Carefully transfer the contents of the pan to a blender or food processor. Let cool for about 10 minutes.

4   Add the salt, sugar and vinegar. Pulse until chunky or blend until smooth according to preference. If you don't have a food processor, it's equally delicious just as it is.

5   Pour into a container and let cool completely before serving. Store in a glass jar out of the fridge for 2–3 months.

i   Or any dried red chilli or chilli
    flakes you can find.

Todos Santos, Baja California Sur, Mexico, shot on a Sony a6500 with a Mitakon Zonghyi fixed 35mm lens

Beetroot/Beet & Almond Dip

This dip is amazing on salads, sarmies and faladels (see Falafel Schnitzels with Cashew Cheese Sauce on page 236).

YOU WILL NEED

1 small cooked beetroot/beet, peeled and quartered

150g/5¼oz/1 cup almonds, soaked overnight

2 tbsp lemon/lime juice

75ml/2½fl oz/⅓ cup water

1 garlic clove

1 tbsp tahini

2 tbsp olive oil

salt and pepper

TO SERVE

small handful of flaked/sliced almonds, toasted

sprinkle of black sesame seeds

drizzle of olive oil

METHOD

1   In a food processor, blend all the ingredients until smooth and creamy, slowly adding more water to reach the desired consistency.

2   Serve topped with toasted flaked/sliced almonds, black sesame seeds and olive oil.

Peanut Dipping Sauce

with ginger, chilli, soy sauce and lime

This works beautifully as a dressing over Asian-inspired salads or vegetables, or as a dip for crudités or summer rolls (see Vietnamese Rice Paper Rolls on page 256).

YOU WILL NEED

handful of peanuts, roasted

thumb-sized piece of root ginger

juice of I lime

I red chilli, deseeded

I tsp coconut sugar/agave

75ml/2½fl oz/⅓ cup water (or more as needed)

2 tbsp liquid aminos/soy sauce

METHOD

I   Blend the ingredients together until smooth and creamy. Add more water as needed depending on whether you're using it as a dip or a dressing.

Creamy Mushroom Sauce
with white wine, garlic, thyme and nuts or seeds

I love making this mushroom sauce with a combination of shimeji, shiitake and oyster mushrooms for depth of flavour, but any mushrooms would work well. Sunflower seeds, when blended with water, produce a seed cream that thickens beautifully when heated – this usually happens quite quickly so keep an eye on it and add more water if neccessary to loosen the sauce and reach your desired consistency.

You can make this mushroom sauce with any nut milk if you don't have cashews or sunflower seeds. Add 1 tablespoon of flour to the mushrooms and slowly stir in 250–500ml/9–17fl oz/1–2 cups of milk over a low heat. The sauce will thicken; add a little more milk as needed. If you are using cashews, soak them beforehand. Overnight is ideal but a quick soak in boiling water for 15–30 minutes will suffice.

YOU WILL NEED

1 onion, diced

2 tbsp olive oil, plus extra to serve

200g/7oz/2 cups mushrooms, sliced

4 garlic cloves, diced

handful of cashew nuts/sunflower seeds

200ml/7fl oz/¾ cup water (or more as needed)

1 tbsp lemon/lime juice

1 tsp Dijon mustard

1 tsp nutritional yeast (optional)

125ml/4fl oz/½ cup wine

a few sprigs of fresh thyme

salt and pepper, to taste

METHOD

1 In a frying pan on a medium-high heat, sauté the onions in the olive oil for 2–3 minutes until translucent, then add the mushrooms and garlic and cook until browned and a little sticky, around 7 minutes.

2 Meanwhile, toast the cashews or sunflower seeds in a dry frying pan on a low heat for 3–5 minutes until golden. Blend together the nuts/seeds, water, lemon/lime juice, mustard and nutritional yeast until smooth and creamy.

3 Add the wine to the mushrooms and allow the alcohol to cook off for a few minutes before turning the heat down to low.

4 Add the nut/seed mixture to the mushrooms and cook through on a low heat 2–4 minutes until the sauce thickens. Slowly add more water to loosen the sauce if it thickens too much.

5 Add some fresh thyme, a drizzle of olive oil and salt and pepper to taste, then serve with your favourite dishes. Spoon it over pasta or chickpea schnitzels, lather it onto veggies or eat it just as it is.

Black Sesame Tahini

*Tahini is my ultimate staple for making sauces and
dressings and adding to veggies or salads. This black
sesame seed tahini is no different. I lather it on everything
and love the dramatic charcoal colour. I particularly
love it served with tortilla strips fried in coconut oil.
To turn it into a delicious dressing, simply combine a
tablespoon of the tahini with a generous squeeze of lemon
juice, a teaspoon of agave, salt, pepper and water as needed.*

*Black sesame seeds may be small, but they are loaded
with nutrients. They are rich in B vitamins such as
thiamine and vitamin E, minerals like copper, manganese,
selenium, molybdenum, zinc, iron, phosphorus, calcium
and magnesium, as well as tryptophan, an amino acid.*

YOU WILL NEED

325g/11½oz/2 cups black sesame seeds (i)
125ml/4fl oz/½ cup olive oil

METHOD

1   Lightly toast the sesame seeds in a dry frying pan on
a medium heat for around 5 minutes or until fragrant.
Pour them into a high-speed food processor and grind
until really fine.

2   Once the sesame seeds begin to stick to the sides of
the food processor, slowly begin adding the olive oil
and process on high until smooth and you have reached
the desired consistency, which should be thick but
pourable.

NOTE

i   Or white sesame seeds if you can't find black, although these won't
give the tahini its charcoal colour.

Carrot Top Chimichurri

You can use any herbs in this recipe, but the beauty of using the tops of your carrots (which you can buy from your local farmer's market) is that you have zero waste and they also happen to taste really delicious – so much so that it seems crazy that we ever throw them away in the first place.

YOU WILL NEED

30g/1oz/1 cup carrot tops, very finely chopped

2 garlic cloves, finely chopped

4 tbsp olive oil

1 tbsp red wine vinegar

1 tsp agave nectar

1 tsp dried oregano

salt and pepper, to taste

METHOD

1   Mix all the ingredients together in a bowl until well combined.

Cashew Nut Labneh

with rosemary and black salt

YOU WILL NEED

300g/10½oz/2 cups cashew nuts, soaked overnight (i)

4 tbsp cornstarch/tapioca

400ml/14fl oz/1⅔ cups hot water

1 tbsp lemon juice

4 tbsp nutritional yeast

pinch of salt

couple of ice cubes

350ml/13fl oz olive oil

a few sprigs of fresh rosemary

handful of rosemary flowers

a few pinches of black salt

METHOD

1 In a food processor, blend the cashew nuts, cornstarch/
   tapioca, hot water, lemon juice, yeast, salt and ice cubes on
   high until smooth and creamy.

2 Pour the mixture into a saucepan and cook on a medium
   heat for 10 minutes, continuously whisking while the mixture
   thickens. Remove from the heat and allow to cool.

3 Prepare a bowl of icy water. Place spoonfuls of the mixture
   into the cold water and allow to set for 2–5 minutes.

4 Meanwhile, prepare a 750ml/26fl oz jar by filling it halfway
   with olive oil, then add sprigs of rosemary, a handful of
   rosemary flowers and a few pinches of black salt.

5 Transfer the labneh balls to the jar of olive oil and store in the
   fridge. You could also roll each labneh ball in za'atar, spices
   or mixed herbs for a variety of flavours.

NOTE

i If you don't have time, quickly soak the
   cashews in boiling water for 15 minutes.

81

Healing Elixirs

These magical potions are a testament to the incredible healing power of plants. Drinking these elixirs every day improves your intake of essential nutrients and minerals that are released when plants steep in water or milk. Try the Mint & Cinnamon Tea on page 84 for a pick me up in the morning and the Golden Milk Latte on page 99 to ease inflammation and encourage a peaceful night's sleep.

Healing Elixirs

SPICY MASALA CHAI

The spices in chai aid digestion and ginger helps with nausea.

500ml/17fl oz/2 cups water
thumb-sized piece of
  root ginger, sliced
4 cloves
4 cardamom pods
1–2 cinnamon sticks
¼ tsp fennel seeds
4 whole black peppercorns
1–2 black/rooibos tea bags
  (or 1–2 tsp loose leaf tea)
125ml/4fl oz/½ cup milk
1 tsp sweetener, to taste

Place all the ingredients in a saucepan except for the milk and sweetener. Heat on a medium heat until the mixture boils and then simmer for 10 minutes. Strain and add the milk and sweetener to serve.

GINGER, HONEY & LEMON

This brew is amazing for cold and flu season.

thumb-sized piece of
  root ginger, sliced
500ml/17fl oz/2 cups water
juice of 1 lemon
⅓ tsp cayenne pepper
1–2 tsp honey

Put the ginger, water, lemon juice and cayenne into a saucepan over a low heat. Simmer for 5–10 minutes and then add the honey to taste.

ROSEMARY TEA

Works like a dream for headaches, digestion and cramps. Serves 2–4.

handful of rosemary leaves
1 litre/34fl oz/4 cups water

Put the rosemary and water into a small pan over a low heat. Simmer for 5–10 minutes until infused.

MINT & CINNAMON TEA

Cinnamon regulates blood sugar and mint has anti-inflammatory properties.

couple sprigs of mint
stick of cinnamon

Place the cinnamon and mint in a mug or tea pot and fill with boiled water. Allow to steep for 5 minutes and enjoy. You can keep topping up with boiled water all day.

HIBISCUS, ORANGE & MINT ICE TEA

1 cup of hibiscus tea provides your recommended daily iron.

4 tbsp dried hibiscus
1 litre/35fl oz/4¼ cups
  freshly boiled water
2 oranges, sliced
handful of mint leaves
1 tbsp coconut sugar/agave
ice

Steep the hibiscus in the water for 5 minutes, then strain and allow to cool. Serve in a jug with orange slices, mint, coconut sugar/agave and ice.

CACAO, CINNAMON & CHILLI LATTE

Cacao is rich in antioxidants, flavonoids and magnesium.

2 tsp cacao powder
1 tsp coconut sugar/agave
pinch of chilli powder
sprinkle of cinnamon
250ml/9fl oz/1 cup of milk

Combine all the ingredients in a saucepan and warm through over a medium heat while whisking continuously. Once it begins to froth and bubble, remove from heat. This can happen quickly so keep an eye on it to prevent boiling over.

ROOIBOS & PASSIONFRUIT ICE TEA

Granadillas/passionfruit may have a calming effect, are high in antioxidants and boost immunity.

4 rooibos teabags
1 litre/34fl oz/4 cups water
2 granadillas/passionfruit,
  halved and deseeded
ice
jasmine flowers

Steep the teabags in the water for 5 minutes. Remove the teabags and allow to cool. Serve in a jug with the granadillas/passionfruit, ice and jasmine flowers.

Somewhere on the road between Srinagar and Leh, Northern India, shot on a Panasonic GH4 with a fixed 50mm lens

Bougainvillea, Ginger, Lime & Rosemary Tea

Bougainvillea flowers are anti-inflammatory and act as a body detoxifier. They can be helpful for sore throats, ulcers and coughs.

YOU WILL NEED

2 sprigs of rosemary
thumb-sized piece of root ginger
couple of slices of lime/lemon
handful of bougainvillea petals (i)

METHOD

1   Place all the ingredients in a jar and fill with boiling water.

2   Steep for 10 minutes.

3   Strain and serve either hot or cold.

NOTE

i   You could also use the petals from chamomile, lavender, calendula, rose or lemon balm flowers.

Beetroot/ Beet Latte

with reishi mushroom and cardamom

YOU WILL NEED

250ml/9fl oz/1 cup boiling water
4–6 cardamom pods
250ml/9fl oz/1 cup coconut milk
2 tsp beetroot/beet powder
2 tsp reishi mushroom powder (optional)

METHOD

1   Mix the boiling water and cardamom pods in a saucepan over a low heat. Gently simmer for 5–20 minutes for a lighter to more robust infusion.

2   Add the coconut milk, beetroot/beet powder and reishi mushroom powder (if using) and whisk continuously until the powders have dissolved. Serve with a dusting of cinnamon and dried rose petals.

Homemade Coconut Milk

Coconut milk is a rich source of manganese, phosphorus and iron and can be used as a hair conditioner, in face washes and cleansers and on skin for sunburn.

I learned from a wonderful Sri Lankan lady how to make coconut milk from scratch. She used this amazing tool for removing the flesh from the coconut, which makes the whole process a lot quicker.

I've modified the recipe so that you can make it anywhere you have a blender and a nut milk cloth or sieve. Use older, browner coconuts.

This method works equally well with any nuts, seeds or oats, soaked overnight. When using oats, be sure to use steel-cut oats and do not over blend, as this can result in a very gooey milk. When using cashew nuts, it is not necessary to strain it. For a super-quick nut milk, blend 1–2 teaspoons of nut butter with 250ml/9fl oz/1 cup of warm water.

1   *Start by turning the coconut around to look for the three holes. Using a screwdriver or strong small knife, poke to see which hole is easiest to open. Once open, pour the coconut water into a glass.*

2   *Place the coconut in a clean towel to prevent it from rolling around and to protect your surfaces. Make sure the definite ridges in the husk of the coconut are running vertically. Hold the coconut firmly and use the back of a heavy chef's knife or cleaver to tap around the equator (the middle) of the coconut. Gently tap in a circular motion, gradually increasing the force. You'll feel the coconut starting to crack. Be careful not to hit too hard to avoid shattering the coconut into many pieces.*

3   *You will need a knife to cut the white coconut flesh out of its shell (this will come to approximately 1 cup of flesh). Half a coconut is enough to make about 1 litre/ 35fl oz/4¼ cups of milk.*

4   *Place the coconut flesh in a blender and fill with warm water (about 1 litre/35fl oz/4¼ cups). If you don't have access to fresh coconuts, you can use 1 cup of dried coconut flakes instead.*

5   *Allow to soak for at least 10 minutes to release the oils before blending on high for about 2 minutes. Pour the liquid into a bowl through a nut milk cloth and squeeze out every drop.*

JOURNAL ENTRY //

I've been thinking about what it means to come home – and how it feels to me – to be less about a specific place and more about the home in which we physically house ourselves: our mind, body and soul and what it means to feel at home in each of these. Because you can live in the most beautiful place in the world and still feel unfulfilled. Maybe it's about giving more and expecting less – of yourself and others. And engaging in acts that feed those three important aspects of ourselves. The balance, the ebb and flow, the cycles of nature, the rhythms of the earth, feeling the beings of this world, this entire universe. A speck of dust in a never ending and ever expanding cosmos.

Baja, California Sur, shot on a Sony a6500 with a Mitakon Zhongyi fixed 35mm lens.

Coconut & Cardamom Iced Coffee

with homemade nut milk

This coffee is absolute bliss. If you don't like coconut milk, you can substitute with your favourite milk to make this beauty. Adding cardamom gives it a delicious spicy lift and helps with the acidity levels of the coffee. Use 2 cardamom pods per serving of coffee.

YOU WILL NEED

coffee beans

2 cardamom pods (i)

a splash of Homemade Coconut Milk
   (see page 91)

sprinkle of ground cinnamon

METHOD

1   When you grind your coffee, add the cardamom pods.

2   Make your coffee as you usually would. Leave to cool.

3   Fill a jar or glass with ice and pour the cooled coffee over.

4   Finish off with homemade nut milk and a sprinkle of cinnamon.

NOTE

i   By adding cardamom to coffee, you can actually neutralize the acidity of coffee. Cardamom helps with digestion, detoxification and blood pressure, and even has anti-inflammatory properties.

Rose Maca Latte

YOU WILL NEED

250ml/9fl oz/1 cup water
1 cinnamon stick
2 tbsp dried rose petals
250ml/9fl oz/1 cup coconut milk
2 tsp maca powder

METHOD

1   Pour the water into a small pan and add the cinnamon and rose petals. Gently simmer for 5–20 minutes for a lighter to more robust infusion.

2   Strain to remove the cinnamon and rose petals. Add the infusion back to the pot with the coconut milk and maca and whisk until warmed through.

Golden Milk Latte

This golden milk is a potent health tonic and the ideal elixir to drink before bed.

YOU WILL NEED

250ml/9fl oz/1 cup water
1 tsp grated fresh turmeric (i)
1 tsp grated fresh root ginger (ii)
pinch of black pepper
1 cinnamon stick
250ml/9fl oz/1 cup milk
1 tsp sweetener of choice

METHOD

1   Pour the water into a small pan and add the remaining ingredients apart from the milk and sweetener. Heat until the mixture boils and then turn down the heat and gently simmer for 5–20 minutes for a lighter to more robust infusion. Add the milk and warm through for another minute.

2   Strain, add your favourite sweetener and enjoy.

NOTES

i   Or 1 tsp ground turmeric.

ii   Or 1 tsp ground ginger.

Break the Fast

Break your fast healthily with the colourful and nutritious recipes in this chapter. Since so many breakfasts center around eggs, I have included delicious high protein alternatives for you to explore, such as the Chickpea Flour Omelette on page 112, the most delicious gluten free Blueberry Buckwheat Pancakes on page 107 and a scrumptious Shakshuka on page 115.

Smoothie Bowls

Smoothie bowls are the perfect way to incorporate adaptogen powders such as maca, ashwagandha and moringa into your breakfast. I always use a base of frozen banana chunks to really get that creamy texture going, and then the options of what you can add are endless: kale, spinach, courgettes/zucchini, avocado, any frozen or fresh fruit, any milk, nut butters and nuts. Go wild, tap into your creativity and experiment with flavours and colours. The below recipe will serve 1 bowl.

YOU WILL NEED

2 bananas, cut into pieces and frozen

2 handfuls frozen blueberries

1 tbsp nut butter

125ml/4fl oz/½ cup milk

1 tsp cacao powder/nibs

TOPPINGS

any nuts

any seeds

fresh/dried fruits

dried coconut chips

cacao nibs

edible flowers

nut butters

METHOD

1   In a blender or food processor, blend all the ingredients together until smooth and creamy.

2   Serve with your favourite topping combinations – here I topped with fresh coconut, hemp hearts, black sesame seeds and moringa.

Vegan Crumpets

with coconut yoghurt, goji berries and nut butter

serves 2–4
cooking time: 15 minutes

These crumpets are simple, light, fluffy and nutritious. They are delicious with blueberries, hemp hearts and coconut cream or cacao nibs, raspberries or strawberries, toasted nuts and mint, and drizzled with maple syrup.

YOU WILL NEED

120g/4¼oz/1 cup flour of your choice
2 tbsp coconut sugar
1 tbsp baking powder
½ tsp salt
250ml/9fl oz/1 cup milk
1 tbsp apple cider vinegar
1 tsp vanilla extract
1 tbsp coconut oil
1 tbsp coconut yogurt
1 tbsp nut butter
handful of goji berries

METHOD

1   In a medium bowl, add the flour, sugar, baking powder and salt, and stir to combine.

2   In a separate bowl, add the milk, apple cider vinegar and vanilla, and stir to combine.

3   Pour the liquid mixture into the dry mixture and whisk until smooth.

4   In a large frying pan on a medium heat, fry spoonfuls of the mixture (4–6 crumpets) in coconut oil and wait until bubbles appear on the surface before flipping and cooking the other side, about 2 minutes each side. You might have to make the crumpets in batches depending on the size of your pan.

5   Top with the coconut yogurt, nut butter and goji berries and serve.

104

Blueberry Buckwheat Pancakes

makes 6–12 pancakes
cooking time: 15 minutes, plus resting time

Did you know that buckwheat is actually a seed? It's high in protein and gluten free and a fantastic grain and flour alternative. Simply pulse dried hulled buckwheat in a food processor to make your own flour. I use cooked buckwheat in salads, soups and stews, or blended with coconut milk, cinnamon and cardamom for a delicious porridge.

I like to serve these pancakes with maple syrup, toasted coconut, banana slices and some fresh passionfruit/granadilla.

METHOD

1 In a large bowl, combine all the dry ingredients and then mix in the liquid ingredients until a smooth batter is formed. Add the blueberries, then leave the batter to rest in the fridge for 10 minutes.

2 Once rested, remove the batter from the refrigerator. If the mixture feels too thick, you can add water to loosen it.

3 Melt the coconut oil in a large frying pan on a medium heat. Add spoonfuls of the mixture to the pan and cook for approximately 2 minutes until tiny bubbles form on the surface. Flip, then cook the other side, about 2 minutes. You may need to do this in batches depending on the size of the pan.

4 Enjoy with your favourite toppings.

YOU WILL NEED

120g/4¼oz/1 cup buckwheat flour
2½ tsp baking powder
¼ tsp sea salt
1 tsp ground cinnamon
250ml/9fl oz/1 cup milk
1 tbsp lemon juice
1 tsp vanilla extract
2 tbsp maple syrup
75g/2⅔oz/½ cup blueberries
    (optional)
1 tsp coconut oil

TOPPINGS

any nuts and/or seeds
fresh/dried fruits
dried coconut chips
cacao nibs
edible flowers
nut butters
honey/maple syrup

*East Cape, San Jose del Cabo, Baja California Sur, shot on
a Sony a6500 with a Mitakon Zhongyi fixed 35mm lens*

Herbed Chickpea Pancakes

with greens, avocado and a beetroot/beet, ginger and lemon sauce

serves 2
cooking time: 15 minutes

These pancakes are so easy to make, high in protein and absolutely mouth-watering. I serve them with avocado, rocket/arugula, nasturtiums and a tangy, sour and sweet beetroot/beet and ginger dressing. They are so good for breakfast, or any time really. You could try them with the Jackfruit on page 222, Falafel Schnitzels on page 236 or the Beetroot/Beet Balls on page 186.

METHOD

1 Place the chickpea flour, baking powder, water, herbs, olive oil, salt and pepper in a blender and combine until smooth and creamy.

2 Heat some oil in a large frying pan and pour in some of the mixture until the bottom of the pan is covered. Cook for 2–4 minutes until bubbles form on the surface, then flip and cook the other side, about 2–4 minutes. Repeat with the remaining mixture to make 4–6 pancakes. You could also fry spoonfuls of the mixture for smaller crumpet-style pancakes.

3 Serve with the toppings I have suggested and try some of the other delicious sauces from the Dressed Up section (pages 40–81).

YOU WILL NEED

120g/4¼oz/1 cup chickpea flour
1 tsp baking powder
250ml/9fl oz/1 cup water
handful of fresh green herbs
1 tbsp olive oil, plus extra for frying
salt and pepper

TOPPINGS

½ avocado, sliced
handful of rocket/arugula
nasturtium flowers
1 chilli, sliced
Beetroot/Beet, Ginger & Lemon
   Sauce (see page 53)

Chickpea Flour Omelette

with kale & green olives

serves 2
cooking time: 10 minutes

I had been exploring not eating eggs for health reasons and what I could make in their place and I had started to miss some of the meals I made with eggs. Then I found beautiful replacements like chickpea flour. This omelette is really high in plant protein and full of powerful ingredients like turmeric (for inflammation), kale (for iron and energy) and olives (good fats for the skin). Some of my favourite combinations are mushroom and spinach; tomato and basil; or asparagus, lemon zest and mint.

YOU WILL NEED

2 heaped tbsp chickpea flour
pinch of ground turmeric
1 tsp salt and 1 tsp pepper
250ml/9fl oz/1 cup water
1 tbsp olive oil
2 handfuls of kale leaves, stems removed and broken into pieces
½ red onion, chopped
1 garlic clove, chopped
handful of olives, sliced

METHOD

1   Put the chickpea flour, turmeric, salt and pepper into a large bowl and mix. Gradually add the water while mixing with a whisk or fork. The mixture should resemble the consistency of beaten egg.

2   In a frying pan on a medium heat, sauté the rest of the ingredients in olive oil for 5 minutes until lightly browned.

3   Slowly add the chickpea mixture, turn the heat to low and put the lid on for 5–7 minutes until cooked through, then serve.

112

Shakshuka

with hummus, pesto and chilli oil pita breads

serves 2–4
cooking time: 30 minutes

I'm in love with this rich tomato deliciousness topped with a few of my favourite things. Soak up the goodness with tasty chilli oil pitas and creamy hummus. Shakshuka is traditionally eggs baked in a rich tomato sauce but here I've swapped the eggs for tofu, chickpeas/garbanzo beans or mushrooms.

METHOD

1   In a pan on a medium heat, fry the onion, garlic, smoked paprika and 1 teaspoon of cumin in 2 tablespoons of olive oil for about 5 minutes until golden.

2   Add the green or red pepper and sauté for 2–3 more minutes, before throwing in the canned tomatoes and coconut sugar, then season with salt and pepper. Turn the heat down and allow to simmer for 10 minutes.

3   In the meantime, heat the grill/broiler. Spread the chickpeas/garbanzo beans, tofu or mushrooms out on a baking sheet, add the remaining 1 tbsp of oil and cumin and the coriander, season with salt and pepper, then mix to coat. Grill in the oven for 20–25 minutes, turning half way through to ensure even cooking.

4   Mix the chopped chillies with 1 tablespoon of olive oil. Brush the pitas with the oil before lightly toasting in a pan on a medium heat for 3 minutes on either side until golden.

5   To serve, place spoonfuls of the tomato sauce onto a plate or bowl, add the grilled chickpeas, tofu or mushrooms, scatter over fresh parsley, coriander/cilantro or basil leaves and add your favourite toppings (which you have stored in jars in the fridge because you are now a badass Nigella).

YOU WILL NEED

1 onion, diced

1 garlic clove, diced

1 tsp smoked paprika

2 tsp ground cumin

3 tbsp olive oil, plus 1 tbsp for the pitas

1 green or red pepper, deseeded and sliced

400g/14oz can of chopped tomatoes

1 tsp coconut sugar

salt and pepper

400g/14oz can of chickpeas/garbanzo beans or 300g/10½oz block of tofu, cut into cubes, or 2 large handfuls of mushrooms, sliced

1 tsp ground coriander

2 chillies, chopped

2–4 pita breads

handful of parsley, coriander/cilantro or basil leaves

TOPPINGS

Basil Pesto (see page 57)

Creamy Hummus (see page 279)

Smoky Coconut Bacon (see page 40)

Leh, Ladakh, India, shot on a Panasonic GH4 with a fixed 50mm lens

Greenhouse Breakfast

with chickpea cutlets, coconut bacon, tomato and green pepper sauce & sauerkraut

serves 4
cooking time: 20 minutes

This is a meat-free take on a classic farmhouse breakfast, with balanced protein, gut-healing sauerkraut, crispy and smoky coconut bacon, bitter rocket/arugula and thinly sliced fried potatoes.

YOU WILL NEED

I tbsp olive/coconut/avocado oil
Sunshine Sauerkraut (see page 36)
Smoky Coconut Bacon (see page 40)
handful of rocket/arugula
handful of thinly sliced fried potatoes

FOR THE CHICKPEA CUTLETS

400g/14oz can of chickpeas/garbanzo
    beans, drained and rinsed
I tbsp nutritional yeast
I garlic clove
I tsp ground cumin

I tsp ground coriander
I tbsp nut/rice flour
salt and pepper

FOR THE TOMATO AND GREEN PEPPER SAUCE

I green pepper, deseeded and sliced
I tbsp olive oil
400g/14oz can of chopped tomatoes
    or 4 medium tomatoes, chopped
I tsp coconut sugar/agave
salt and pepper

METHOD

1   Preheat the oven to 180°C/350°F/Gas 4 and grease an ovenproof dish with oil.

2   Pulse the chickpea cutlet ingredients in a food processor until it resembles a smooth paste. Shape the mixture into 4 patties with your hands, place in the greased dish and bake until golden, around 15–20 minutes.

3   In a pan on a medium heat, fry the green pepper in olive oil until browned, around 5–10 minutes. Add the tomatoes, sugar, salt and pepper, then turn down the heat to low and allow to simmer for about 10 minutes. Add water as needed.

4   Serve the chickpea cutlets with the tomato and green pepper sauce, sauerkraut topped with coconut bacon, rocket/arugula and thinly sliced fried potatoes.

Skillet Potato Rosti

with steamed asparagus, grilled beetroot/beets and hollandaise sauce

serves 2
cooking time: 20 minutes

This rosti was a total fluke – I discovered it by sheer chance. What emerged from the oven was the most crunchy, delicious, golden potato dream I'd had in a long time. It would work really well on hot coals too and is perfect for a campfire.

YOU WILL NEED

olive oil

handful of asparagus spears, ends removed

1 beetroot/beet, thinly sliced

FOR THE ROSTI

2 potatoes, peeled and grated

2 tbsp chickpea/rice/nut flour

1 tbsp olive oil

½ red onion, grated

FOR THE HOLLANDAISE SAUCE

1 tsp Dijon mustard

1 tbsp olive oil

2 tbsp water

2 tbsp lemon juice

⅓ tsp ground turmeric

salt and black pepper

METHOD

1   Preheat the oven to 220°C/425°F/Gas 7. Pour a thin layer of olive oil into a cast iron pan.

2   Soak the grated potato in water for 20 minutes and then drain. Place the potatoes in a cloth and squeeze out the excess water. In a bowl, mix the ingredients for the rosti. Add the mixture to the pan and press down to form a pan-sized rosti. Bake in the oven for 15 minutes.

3   Meanwhile, whisk the hollandaise ingredients together.

4   Steam the asparagus in a steamer for 5–8 minutes until tender but still with a bit of bite.

5   Brush the beetroot/beet slices with olive oil and pan-fry on a medium heat until lightly charred, around 2 minutes each side.

6   To serve, layer the asparagus and beetroot slices on top of the rosti and drizzle with hollandaise sauce.

Morgan's Bay, Eastern Cape, South Africa, shot on a Canon 5D with a fixed 50mm lens

There's something magical about a bowl of soup that warms the soul, nourishes the body and uplifts the spirit. Whether rich and creamy or a light broth, soups are always comforting: a wholesome meal that feels like a warm hug. While a lot of soups are a lengthy labour of love, most of the soups in this chapter are made in under 30 minutes. I suggest trying some of the crunchy toppings from the Dressed Up section (see pages 40–81) on these soups, such as Smoky Coconut Bacon or Fried Nut and Seed Mix (see page 40) and Mediterranean Dream or Savoury Granola (see page 42).

Soulful Soups

Cosmic Soup

with purple cauliflower and purple sweet potatoes, cashew cream, mint and pistachios

serves 2–4
cooking time: 30 minutes, plus cooling time

I was completely blown away by how this magical purple soup changed from a lavender hue to cerise pink when I added drops of lime to finish it off. This wildly beautiful bowl of art made me realize that every meal really is medicine and should be this eye-catching, healthy, tasty and healing.

When I first made this soup, I was living in Baja California Sur, Mexico, and was lucky enough to have access to the most beautiful and colourful heirloom veggies you could ever dream of. On this particular day, I had been wanting to make purple cauliflower soup and ended up finding a magical purple sweet potato too. What transpired was a cosmic purple bowl of goodness that made me feel as if I was on mild hallucinogens, and the taste and texture almost had me in tears.

If you don't have access to heirloom veggies, standard cauliflower and sweet potato will do.

METHOD

1 Place the sweet potatoes in a saucepan on a medium heat, cover with the water and simmer for 12 minutes. Add the cauliflower to the saucepan and continue to simmer for a further 8 minutes until both the sweet potatoes and cauliflowers florets are tender.

2 Remove from the heat and set aside, allowing the vegetables to cool in the cooking water

3 Place the veggies and half the cooking water in a blender and purée until smooth.

4 Stir in a good glug of olive oil and season with salt and pepper, adding more water if necessary.

5 In a food processor, blend all the cashew cream ingredients until smooth and creamy with a pourable consistency.

6 Serve the cosmic soup with swirls of cashew cream, fresh mint, pistachios and drops of lemon or lime juice.

YOU WILL NEED

2 purple sweet potatoes/yams, peeled and chopped
I head purple cauliflower, broken into florets
I litre/35fl oz/4¼ cups water
olive oil
salt and pepper

FOR THE CASHEW CREAM

75g/2⅔oz/½ cup cashew nuts, soaked overnight (i)
2 tbsp lemon/lime juice
I large garlic clove
75ml/2½fl oz/⅓ cup water
I tsp nutritional yeast (optional)
salt and pepper, to taste

TO SERVE

handful of fresh mint leaves
handful of shelled pistachios
squeeze of lemon/lime juice

NOTE

i   Or if you're short on time, a quick soak in boiling water for 15–30 minutes does the job too.

Sweet Potato, Coconut & Ginger Soup

topped with pearl barley, spring onions/scallions and edible flowers

serves 4
cooking time: 30 minutes

This soup is beautifully creamy and uplifting with the spicy ginger and silky coconut milk. I really adore toppings on a soup, even something simple can transform the dish. Here I used barley, spring onions/scallions, edible flowers and some paprika for a little zing. Sweet potatoes are incredibly high in vitamin A; they support healthy vision and brain function as well as healthy digestion.

METHOD

1 In a large saucepot on a medium heat, fry the onion and ginger in olive oil for 5 minutes until golden brown. Add the turmeric, black pepper and the sweet potatoes and stir through.

2 Pour in the vegetable stock and coconut milk and simmer until the sweet potatoes are soft, around 20 minutes.

3 Remove from the heat and add the lemon juice and a pinch of salt. Pour into a blender and blend until smooth and creamy.

4 Top with pearl barley, spring onions/scallions, edible flowers and paprika and a few good glugs of olive oil.

YOU WILL NEED

1 onion, chopped
thumb-sized piece of root ginger
2 tbsp olive oil, plus more to serve
1 tsp ground turmeric
black pepper (your choice how much)
4 medium sweet potatoes, peeled and
    cut into chunks
750ml/26fl oz/3¼ cups vegetable
    stock
250ml/9fl oz/1 cup coconut milk
juice of 1 lemon
salt

TO SERVE

160g/5⅔oz/1 cup cooked pearl barley
2 spring onions/scallions, finely
    chopped
a few edible flowers
sprinkle of paprika

Spicy Coconut Laksa

with seasonal veggies and crispy coconut bacon

serves 1
cooking time: 20 minutes

This soup is wonderfully simple to make and very light and uplifting in nature. There is something so comforting about slurping a delicious broth with all the right spices, veggies and noodles, and a delectable little crunch to top it all off. This is quick, fresh, fragrant and so tasty!

METHOD

1   In a large saucepan on a medium heat, sauté the spring onion/scallion, garlic, turmeric, red chilli flakes, coriander seeds and ginger in 1 tablespoon of coconut oil for 2 minutes until fragrant.

2   Add the mushrooms, pepper (or any other veg you have) and sesame seeds, and sauté for 2 minutes. Add the noodles, coconut milk and water, bring to the boil and then simmer for 5 mins.

3   Meanwhile, make the coconut bacon. In a pan over a medium heat, lightly fry the coconut slices or chips in the remaining tablespoon of coconut oil and a pinch of salt for 3–5 minutes until golden brown.

4   To serve the soup, squeeze in the lime juice and soy sauce and add salt and white pepper to taste. Garnish with fresh mint, coriander/cilantro or spring onions/scallions and more sesame seeds, and top with the coconut bacon.

NOTES

i   This is a suggestion; any veggies you have will work well.

ii   If you don't have coconut milk, you can use a handful of sesame seeds and a handful of peanuts blended together with 250ml/9fl oz/1 cup of water.

YOU WILL NEED

1 spring onion/scallion, sliced
1 garlic clove, diced
1 tsp ground turmeric
1 tsp red chilli flakes
1 tsp coriander seeds, crushed
thumb-sized piece of root ginger, sliced
2 tbsp coconut oil
4 large oyster mushrooms, cut into bite-size portions
palm-sized piece of red pepper, chopped (i)
1 tbsp sesame seeds, plus extra to garnish
100g/3½oz/1 cup cooked rice noodles
250ml/9fl oz/1 cup coconut milk (ii)
350ml/12fl oz/1½ cups water
handful of fresh brown coconut slices/ coconut chips

TO GARNISH

juice of 1 lime
soy sauce, to serve
handful of fresh mint leaves
handful of fresh coriander/cilantro leaves or spring onion/scallion slices
salt and white pepper, to taste

Leh, Ladakh, India. Shot on a Panasonic GH4 with a fixed 50mm lens

JOURNAL ENTRY //

In a tiny village in the north of India, I bathed every morning in a temple spring, and every day I ate at a restaurant that stole my heart. It was run by a family who grew their veggies organically on a beautiful piece of land just outside the village.

It was rainy and cool and I sat with my lover eating steaming hot bowls of thukpa (Tibetan noodle soup) with fresh mushrooms and homemade tofu. The noodles were lovingly made by hand in front of our eyes. Delicious momos (Tibetan dumplings) with spinach and potatoes and spicy, hot chai with cardamom warming you to the bone. We watched people coming to and from the temple as the rain plopped down.

Looking up at the mountains and down at the crumbling stone walls surrounding the bathing area of the most magical temple spring, ordering dish after dish of the best food I've ever eaten.

I'm pretty sure we ate there three times a day for a week and every day I ate something as delicious as before, yet unique in every way.

Traditional Tibetan Thukpa

with spinach, mushroom and tofu

serves 2
cooking time: 20 minutes

The combination of veggies, noodles, mushrooms, tofu and spices makes this dish one of my favourites from our three-month trip through India. Thukpa is a traditional Tibetan dish which I tried first in the very north of India in a place called Leh, right on the border of Tibet. Surrounded by the Himalayas, the sounds of temple chants, gongs and prayer bowls filled the streets, while we sat slurping bowls of this delicious soup made lovingly with hand-rolled noodles, homemade tofu and vegetables.

METHOD

1   In a saucepan on a medium heat, fry the cumin, turmeric, asafoetida, chillies, ginger, garlic, tomato and red onion in 1 teaspoon of coconut oil for about 6–7 minutes until softened and fragrant.

2   Add the vegetables (excluding the spinach) and bay leaf and sauté for 5 minutes. Then add the vegetable stock and simmer for a further 5 minutes.

3   In a separate pan, fry up the pieces of tofu in the rest of the coconut oil for 3–5 minutes on either side until golden brown. Remove from the heat, then add the spinach and soy sauce.

4   Ladle the soup over homemade noodles or any kind of rice noodles you can get your hands on. Top with the spinach, tofu, fresh coriander/cilantro and a lime or lemon wedge and serve.

YOU WILL NEED

1 tsp ground cumin

1 tsp ground turmeric

⅛ tsp asafoetida or hing

2 chillies, finely chopped

1 tbsp grated root ginger

1 tbsp finely chopped garlic

1 tomato, quartered

1 red onion, finely chopped

1 tbsp coconut oil

½ green pepper, deseeded and cut into chunks

1 large radish, sliced

1 carrot, peeled and sliced

150g/5¼oz/1 cup peas

1 courgette/zucchini, chopped

handful of mushrooms, quartered

1 bay leaf

1 litre/35fl oz/4¼ cups vegetable stock

handful of tofu cubes

4 large spinach leaves

2 tbsp soy sauce

200g/7oz/2 cups cooked rice noodles

handful of fresh coriander/cilantro leaves

lemon or lime wedges, to serve

Everyday Healing Broth

with turmeric for inflammation

serves 2
cooking time: 25–30 minutes

This is the perfect everyday broth to sip as an immune booster and detoxifier. When you start to feel those familiar aches and pains of the flu, this broth will hold and uplift you.

I serve this with the Salsa Macha on page 66, Ginger, Chilli & Garlic Sauce on page 65 and fire-roasted tomatoes (2 tomatoes, halved and roasted over the fire or in the oven.)

METHOD

1 In a pan over a medium heat, fry the miso paste, ginger, turmeric, garlic and spring onions/scallions in the coconut oil for 1–2 minutes until fragrant.

2 Add the mushrooms and cook for 5 minutes.

3 Add all the remaining ingredients except the spinach/pak choi/bok choy leaves and cover with the vegetable stock. Turn the heat down to low and simmer for 20 minutes, adding the spinach or pak choi/bok choy for the last 3 minutes so that it maintains its lovely green colour.

4 Serve with toasted peanuts, fresh mint, purple cabbage and sauerkraut.

YOU WILL NEED

1 tbsp white miso paste
1 tbsp chopped root ginger
2 tsp ground turmeric
1 tsp grated garlic
2 spring onions/scallions, chopped
2 tbsp coconut oil
handful of mushrooms, quartered
1 large radish, sliced
1 chilli, chopped
juice of 1 lemon/lime
1 litre/35fl oz/4¼ cups vegetable stock
handful of baby spinach/pak choi/bok choy leaves

TO SERVE

handful of toasted peanuts
handful of mint leaves
handful of shredded purple cabbage
Sunshine Sauerkraut (see page 36)

Mushroom & Nori Wonton Soup

with edamame and mint

serves 2
cooking time: 25 minutes

I first ate wonton soup with my best friend in Putney Bridge, London, at a little hole-in-the-wall eatery after a gig one night. I fell in love instantly. I still remember how the texture of the soft wontons in the spicy broth felt and tasted.

This rich mushroom broth is delicious and has a beautiful umami flavour. The salty seaweed, crunchy edamame beans and moreish wontons create a really flavourful and playful dance on your tongue.

YOU WILL NEED

1 onion, finely chopped

4-6 garlic cloves, sliced

1 red chilli, sliced

1 tbsp grated root ginger

1 tbsp coconut oil

200g/7oz/2 cups mushrooms, quartered (i)

1 tomato, blended

1 tsp coconut sugar

1 litre/35fl oz/4¼ cups vegetable stock

juice of 2 limes

2 tbsp liquid aminos/soy sauce

10 veggie wontons

150g/5¼oz/1 cup edamame beans/ garden peas

2 tbsp black sesame seeds

2 sheets of nori (dried seaweed), cut into strips

handful of fresh mint leaves

1 tbsp sesame oil

METHOD

1   In a large saucepan on a medium heat, sauté the onion, garlic, chilli and ginger in the coconut oil for 4–5 minutes until softened. Add the mushrooms and cook until browned, about 5 minutes.

2   Add the blended tomato, coconut sugar and stock. Simmer for 5 minutes.

3   Add the lime juice and liquid aminos and simmer for a further 5 minutes. At this point add the wontons and edamame beans and cook until the wontons have softened, about 5 minutes.

4   Remove from the heat. Divide between two bowls and top with sesame seeds, strips of nori and mint and drizzle with sesame oil.

NOTE

i   You could use portabellini, chestnut/cremini, oyster or shiitake.

Ouma's Bean Soup

in a garlic, tomato broth with spinach and rosemary

serves 4

cooking time: 40 minutes–1 hour

I grew up eating this soup, lovingly made by my Ouma (grandmother). I remember smelling delicious aromas dancing down the passage as the beans cooked, luring me into the kitchen to find out what was on the stove. If you are using dried beans, the trick, according to Ouma, is to cook them on their own first, as they take longer and become tough if cooked with tomatoes. Any bean variety would work with this soup. You could try cannellini, butter, borlotti, black and sugar beans.

METHOD

1   Cook the beans in a pressure cooker for 30 minutes. Alternatively, place in a large saucepan on a medium heat, cover with water and simmer for around 1 hour until tender.

2   Meanwhile, in a frying pan on a medium heat, fry the onions, garlic and rosemary in 2 tablespoons of olive oil for 4–5 minutes until golden brown. Add the chopped celery (stalks only) and carrot and cook for 5 minutes until softened.

3   Add the tomatoes and allow the mixture to cook for a further 5 minutes, then add the beans, celery leaves, stock or water, salt and pepper. Turn the heat down to low and cook for a further 5 minutes. Remove from the heat add the spinach, lemon juice and a drizzle of olive oil, then put the lid on and allow to stand for 5 minutes before serving.

4   Serve with crusty bread and olive oil.

YOU WILL NEED

850g/1lb 14oz/2 cups dried beans of
    your choice, soaked overnight (i)
1 onion, finely chopped
4 garlic cloves, finely chopped
4 sprigs of rosemary, leaves picked
    and chopped
2 celery stalks (including leaves),
    finely chopped
2 tbsp olive oil, plus extra to serve
1 carrot, peeled and finely chopped
2–4 ripe tomatoes, diced
1 litre/35fl oz/4¼ cups vegetable
    stock or water
2 handfuls of baby spinach, chopped
Himalayan salt and pepper
juice of ½ lemon
Crusty bread, to serve

NOTE

i   I use dried red speckled sugar
    beans. Or you can replace this with
    2 x 400g/14oz cans of beans of
    your choice.

Creamy Tom Yum

with rice noodles, oyster mushrooms, coconut milk and peanuts

serves 2
cooking time: 25–30 minutes

I discovered this magical soup in the village of Lonely Beach on Koh Chang Island, in Thailand. I had fallen hard for Thai soups, my favourite being tom yum. At a quaint beach restaurant under the palms, I tasted my first morsel of this mind-blowing dish. The wonderful spicy, sour and sweet flavours filled my bowl along with creamy coconut milk, meaty oyster mushrooms, crunchy peanuts and fresh herbs. I was hooked and remember thinking that I had never tasted anything so delicious. Without a doubt, one of my favourite food memories. Traditionally, the Thai soup with a coconut milk base is called tom kha, but this recipe is a unique combination of tom kha and tom yum.

METHOD

1 Pour the stock into a large saucepan on a high heat and bring to the boil.

2 Add the lemongrass, coriander/cilantro stems, ginger, garlic, tomatoes, lime leaves, lime juice, tamarind and red chillies. Return to the boil, then reduce the heat and simmer for 15–20 minutes.

3 Taste the stock and add as much soy sauce and coconut sugar as is necessary to keep the salty-sour-hot-sweet taste.

4 Tear the mushrooms into bite-sized chunks before adding and simmer for 5 minutes. Remove from the heat and add the coconut milk.

5 Place the cooked noodles into two separate bowls and pour the soup over the noodles.

6 Garnish with mint, coriander/cilantro leaves, spring onions/scallions and crushed peanuts.

YOU WILL NEED

1 litre/35fl oz/4¼ cups vegetable stock

1 stick of lemongrass, bruised and chopped

handful coriander/cilantro leaves and stems separated and chopped

1 tbsp chopped root ginger

1 garlic clove, chopped

handful of cherry tomatoes, halved

4 lime leaves (i)

juice of 1 lime/lemon

1 tsp tamarind paste

1–3 red chillies, sliced in half lengthways

1 tbsp liquid aminos/soy sauce

1 tsp coconut sugar

2 handfuls oyster mushrooms

250ml/9fl oz/1 cup coconut milk

2 handfuls cooked rice noodles

handful of fresh mint leaves

1 spring onion/scallion, chopped

handful of unsalted peanuts, crushed and roasted

NOTE

i Strip the lime leaves from their centre vein and chop.

Lonely Beach, Koh Chang, Thailand, shot on a Sony a6500 with a Mitakon Zonghyi fixed 35mm lens

Asparagus & Avocado Soup

with broccoli and basil pesto

serves 2
cooking time: 15 minutes

This is a go-to for me when feeling tight on time and needing a healthy boost. Asparagus is incredible for the kidneys, acting as a diuretic, and broccoli is one of the highest sources of plant-based iron and vitamins A, B and K. Hemp seeds are a great source of plant-based omega 3 and 6.

METHOD

1 Pour the water over the broccoli and asparagus in a large saucepan, leaving them to soak for about 3–5 minutes. Both veggies should turn an even brighter green. Drain the veggies, setting the soaking water aside. On a high heat, saute the vegetables in olive oil for 3 minutes, adding the garlic for the last 30 seconds to prevent it from burning.

2 Add the veggies and garlic to a blender with the avocado, half the soaking water, lemon juice, olive oil, salt, pepper and most of the seeds (leave some for garnish). Blend until smooth and creamy, adding more water as needed until you reach your desired consistency.

3 It is optional here to add a couple of spoonfuls of coconut cream. Garnish with basil pesto, salt, black pepper and seeds.

NOTE

i   Toast your choice of seeds in a dry pan over a medium heat for 3-5 minutes for a nuttier flavour.

YOU WILL NEED

1 litre/35fl oz/4¼ cups freshly boiled water
1 small head of broccoli, broken into florets
handful of asparagus spears, woody ends removed, chopped
2 garlic cloves, sliced
1 tbsp olive oil, plus a good glug for blending
1 ripe avocado
juice of 1 small lemon/lime
Himalayan salt and black pepper
75g/2⅔oz/½ cup hemp/pumpkin/ sunflower seeds (i)
4 tbsp coconut cream (optional)
Basil Pesto (see page 57), to serve

Lemony Green Soup

with loads of mint, topped with toasted pumpkin seeds and hemp chilli oil

serves 2
cooking time: 20 minutes

I adore this soup as it is incredibly light and fresh and takes very little time to prepare and cook. If you have a NutriBullet RX, simply place the raw ingredients into the large jug and put it on the "heat and extract" setting, wait 7 minutes and voila! If you don't, steam the veg before and then blitz.

METHOD

1 Steam the broccolini for 3 minutes, then add the frozen peas and continue steaming for a further 2 minutes until both are softened but still bright green.

2 Add all the ingredients to the blender and blend on high until smooth and creamy.

3 For the hemp chilli oil, pulse the green chilli in a food processor until chopped.

4 Cover with hemp oil, a squeeze of lemon juice and salt.

5 Top the soup with toasted pumpkin seeds, edible flowers and the chilli oil and another drizzle of lemon juice.

YOU WILL NEED

10 broccolini stalks
300g/10½ oz/2 cups fresh or frozen peas
handful of fresh mint leaves
juice of I lemon
thumb-sized piece of root ginger
750ml/26fl oz/3¼ cups vegetable stock
2 tbsp sunflower seeds, toasted
salt and pepper, to taste

TOPPINGS

I green chilli
a good glug of hemp oil
juice of I lemon
handful of pumpkin seeds, toasted
edible flowers

Courgette/Zucchini & Sundried Tomato Soup

with hemp hearts and microgreens

serves 2
cooking time: 20 minutes

Courgettes/zucchini, sundried tomatoes and olive oil are meant to be eaten together, and this soup is testament to that. It's creamy and tangy, transporting you to a vineyard in Italy with its Mediterranean flavours. The addition of hemp hearts adds a nutty dimension that I adore. Hemp seeds contain the highest amount of plant protein and omega 3 and 6 fats of any plant food. (i)

METHOD

1   In a saucepan over a medium heat, sauté the onion in olive oil for 4–5 minutes until golden and then add the garlic and cook for a further 30 seconds.

2   Throw in the courgettes/zucchini, stirring until lightly browned, about 5 minutes.

3   Add the sundried tomatoes, vegetable stock or water, salt and pepper and simmer for 4–5 minutes until the courgettes have softened but not lost their colour.

4   Remove from the heat and pour into a blender, leaving some of the liquid behind. Add the lemon juice, hemp hearts and thyme and blend until creamy. Add more liquid as needed to reach your desired consistency.

5   Serve each portion topped with more hemp hearts, lemon zest, greens, olive oil, black pepper and sundried tomatoes.

YOU WILL NEED

1 red onion, finely chopped

2 tbsp olive oil, plus extra to serve

2 garlic cloves, finely chopped

2 large or 4 medium courgettes/ zucchini, chopped

60g/2oz/1 cup sundried tomatoes in oil, plus more to serve

1 litre/35fl oz/4¼ cups vegetable stock or water

salt and pepper

zest and juice of 1 lemon

75g/2⅔oz/½ cup hemp hearts, plus more to serve

couple of sprigs of thyme, leaves picked

2 handfuls of greens (ii)

NOTES

i   Hemp hearts are the inner part of the hemp seeds. They are also known as shelled hemp seeds and have a soft texture and a milder, nutty flavor. They are easier to digest.

ii Mint, basil, sunflower micro greens, rocket/arugula and parsley all work well.

Cerritos, Baja California Sur, Mexico, shot on a Sony a6500, Mitakon Zhongyi fixed 35mm lens

Turmeric, Wild Garlic & Cauliflower Soup

with courgettes/zucchini, lemon rind and dukkah

serves 2–4
cooking time: 15 minutes

This soup takes about 15 minutes to make and is so creamy, silky and melt-in-the-mouth that you'll want to eat it over and over again. The dukkah adds a delicious crunch and the lemon rind and wild garlic flowers give that extra zing and colour.

Wild garlic has a much milder flavour than regular garlic. It is rich in antioxidants and has antibacterial, antiviral and anti-inflammatory properties. The purple flowers have the most delicious, sweet garlic flavour.

METHOD

1 In a saucepan over a medium heat, sauté the onion in olive oil for 3–4 minutes until translucent. Add the cauliflower and courgettes/zucchini, turmeric and wild garlic and stir to combine.

2 Cover with water and cook for 10 minutes until the veggies have softened.

3 Remove the pan from the heat and purée using a blender, adding salt and pepper to taste.

4 Divide the soup between bowls. Sprinkle with lemon rind and dukkah and top with wild garlic flowers (or any edible flowers) and a squeeze of lemon juice plus a good glug of olive oil.

YOU WILL NEED

1 onion, finely chopped

2 tbsp olive oil, plus more to serve

1 head cauliflower, broken into florets

4 large courgettes/zucchini, chopped

1 tsp ground turmeric

4 wild garlic sprigs or 2 garlic cloves, chopped

1 litre/35fl oz/4¼ cups water

salt and pepper

4 tsp lemon rind, thinly sliced

Dukkah (see page 40)

juice of 1 lemon

wild garlic flowers or any edible flowers, to decorate (optional)

Vietnamese Pho
with star anise, cinnamon and cloves

serves 2
cooking time: 45 minutes

This soup is the ultimate in wholesome healing goodness. My obsession with Asian broths has led me to discover this perfectly balanced, flavoursome and cleansing broth. It's fresh and light and filled with aromatic spices. Charring the onion and ginger really gives this soup its rich umami flavour.

METHOD

1 Char the onion, ginger and garlic over an open flame or under the grill/broiler for approximately 5 minutes. This is a very important step, as it changes the flavour of the soup to something smoky and caramelized. You want them slightly blackened for flavour.

2 In a large saucepan over a medium heat, bring the vegetable stock to a simmer.

3 Meanwhile, in a dry frying pan over a medium heat, lightly heat the star anise, cloves, cardamom and cinnamon for 3–4 minutes until they begin to release their beautiful aromas.

4 Add the onion, ginger, garlic and spices to the simmering stock. Add the juice of half a lemon, the soy sauce and the chilli. Allow to simmer for 30 minutes.

5 Chop the white parts off the spring onions/scallions and add to the soup, setting the green parts aside for the garnish. Divide the carrots and/or courgettes/zucchini, mangetout/snowpeas and baby corn between two soup bowls. Pour the broth over the raw veggies through a sieve/fine-mesh strainer.

6 Serve with a side of mint, coriander/cilantro, sprouts, the remaining lemon juice, chilli, Sriracha and hoisin so that each person can season their soup accordingly. Adding the fresh herbs at the end allows their flavours to release into the broth without losing their nutrients.

157

YOU WILL NEED

I onion, halved

thumb-sized piece of root ginger, cut into chunks

½ a head of garlic

I litre/35fl oz/4¼ cups vegetable stock

2–3 star anise

4–6 cloves

4 cardamom pods

I cinnamon stick

I lemon/lime

4 tbsp soy sauce/liquid aminos

I green chilli, deseeded and chopped, plus extra for serving if desired

3 spring onions/scallions

2 carrots/courgettes/zucchini, spiralized or grated

handful of mangetout/snow peas, halved lengthways

4 baby corn, halved lengthways

TO SERVE

sprigs of fresh mint and coriander/cilantro

lemon/lime wedge

sprouts (bean/radish)

I green chilli, chopped

Sriracha chilli sauce

hoisin sauce

One Pot Wonders

Cooked in one pot, pan or oven tray, the recipes in this chapter are both functional and tasty. I would start with the One pot Two Bean Chilli on page 180, Butternut Squash Risotto on page 165 or the Lemon Caper Pasta on page 166 before getting a little bit more creative with the Aubergine/Eggplant Sarmie on page 169 by adding your favourite fillings.

Smoky Black Bean Chilli

with red peppers, paprika and coriander/cilantro

serves 4
cooking time: 30 minutes

This dish is inspired by my time in Mexico with its never-ending avocados and wonderful spicy sauces. This black bean chilli can be made using any other beans too. It gets its smokiness from the smoked paprika and the blackened red peppers. I serve this with almond and ginger butternut squash, broccoli in a green herb sauce and chunks of avocado with fresh lime and coriander/cilantro.

METHOD

1   With tongs, hold the red pepper over the gas flame of your hob/stovetop to blacken the outside, about 8–10 minutes. If you do not have a gas hob, put the pepper under a hot grill/broiler, turning occassionally. Once the skin has blackened, cover in a bowl and leave to cool. Peel the skin off once cooled.

2   Heat the oil in a saucepan over a medium heat, add the spices and cook for 1–2 minutes. Add the onion and fry for 5–10 minutes until golden.

3   Throw in the tomatoes, cooled red pepper, garlic, salt and pepper, pour in the water and simmer for 5 minutes. Add the coconut sugar and black beans and continue to simmer for 15–20 minutes (stirring occasionally) until the sauce has reduced by roughly a third.

4   In the meantime, steam the butternut squash for 6–8 minutes, then add the broccoli and steam both for a further 6 minutes until tender. If you don't have a steamer, simply cover the broccoli in boiled water and blanch until the broccoli turns a bright green colour, around 3 minutes. Place the butternut squash in a saucepan, cover with water, bring to the boil and cook for about 10 minutes.

5   Toss the toasted almonds, the cooked butternut, the root ginger, oil and salt and pepper in a bowl to coat and serve.

6   Drizzle the green goddess dressing over the broccoli. Dress the avocado in the lime juice.

7   Plate the chilli with the butternut squash, broccoli and avocado and scatter with fresh coriander/cilantro. Serve with rice if desired.

YOU WILL NEED

1 red pepper
2 tbsp olive oil
1 tbsp ground cumin
1 tbsp ground coriander/cilantro
1 tbsp smoked paprika
1 large onion, finely chopped
4–6 large ripe tomatoes, diced
2 garlic cloves, chopped
salt and pepper, to taste
500ml/17fl oz/2 cups water
1 tsp coconut sugar
2 x 400g/14oz cans of black beans,
    drained and rinsed (i)
1 avocado, cut into chunks
juice of 1 lime
handful of fresh coriander/cilantro
    leaves

FOR THE BUTTERNUT SQUASH

280g/10oz/2 cups butternut squash
    cut into chunks
2 handfuls flaked/sliced almonds,
    toasted
1 tbsp grated fresh root ginger
1 tbsp olive oil
salt and pepper

FOR THE BROCCOLI

350g/12oz/2 cups broccoli florets
Green Goddess Dressing (see page 61)

NOTE

i Or the soaked, cooked equivalent,
   around 500g/17²⁄₃oz/2¾ cups.

Calle de Manuel
Doblado
←

322

JOURNAL ENTRY //
Mexico, I miss your food, your intricately layered sauces and colourful textiles, cobbled streets and fiestas, mezcal with grapefruit and serrano chilli, avocados and limes and all things delectable, cacao and cactuses, jungles, mountains and beaches. Your heartbeat is unique, rhythmical and warm.

Shot on a Sony a6500 with a Mitakon Zhongyi fixed 35mm lens

Butternut Squash Risotto

with cashew cream and and crispy fried sage

serves 4
cooking time: 1 hour

This roasted butternut squash risotto is comfort food at its best – creamy, rich and fragrant when topped with fried sage.

The beauty of this dish is that you do not have to stand over the stove stirring it. Just pop it in the oven and forget about it. You can use any other root vegetable in the same way as the squash.

METHOD

1 Preheat the oven to 200°C/400°F/Gas 6.

2 Spread the butternut squash out in an ovenproof dish, drizzle with half the olive oil and season with salt and pepper. Roast until golden brown, around 20–30 minutes.

3 Meanwhile, in an ovenproof pan on a medium heat, sauté the onion, garlic, carrots and celery in 1 tablespoon of oil for about 7 minutes until lightly browned.

4 Add the Arborio rice and stir for 2–3 minutes until it has a slight golden colour. Add the white wine and simmer for 2–3 minutes, stirring constantly until most of the liquid has evaporated.

5 Add 750ml/26fl oz/3¼ cups of the vegetable stock and stir. Put the lid on and place in the oven (remove the squash at this point). Turn the oven down to 180°C/350°F/Gas 4 and cook for about 45 minutes.

6 Remove the rice from the oven. It will be quite dry, but don't worry. Add the remaining 250ml/9fl oz/1 cup of hot vegetable stock, a drizzle more olive oil and a pinch of red chilli flakes and stir through.

7 Stir in the roasted butternut and some salt and pepper.

8 Lightly fry the sage in olive oil or butter for 30 seconds until crispy.

9 Serve the risotto with fried sage, cashew cream and vegan parmesan.

YOU WILL NEED

1 small butternut squash, cut into
    chunks
3 tbsp olive oil
salt and pepper
1 onion, diced
2 garlic cloves, finely chopped
1 large carrot, peeled and finely
    chopped
2 celery stalks, finely chopped
300g/10½oz/1½ cups Arborio rice
250ml/9fl oz/1 cup white wine
1 litre/35fl oz/4¼ cups vegetable
    stock
pinch of red chilli flakes

TO SERVE

handful of sage leaves, finely chopped
Cashew Cream (see page 126)
Vegan Parm (see page 42)

Lemon Caper Pasta

with a creamy cashew sauce, crispy fried capers and garlic

serves 2
cooking time: 15 minutes

The sauce is made in a blender and then warmed through once the pasta is cooked, making it very simple and quick to prepare. I love these crispy capers so much and have started adding them to salads, soups and pastas for that crunchy, salty kick I crave.

METHOD

1. Cook the pasta in a pan of boiling salted water according to package directions, until al dente. Drain, saving some of the pasta water.

2. Meanwhile, in a blender, combine all the sauce ingredients until smooth, adding more water, if necessary, until the desired consistency is reached (it should resemble the Creamiest "No-Cheese" Sauce on page 49).

3. For the caper breadcrumbs, pulse the sunflower seeds, pumpkin seeds, oregano, lemon zest and paprika into crumbs in a food processor.

4. Heat the olive oil in a frying pan over a medium heat, then add the capers, garlic, the seed mixture, salt and pepper and fry for 3–4 minutes until golden and crispy.

5. Mix the sauce into the pasta and stir well, adding around 125ml/ 4¼fl oz/½ cup of the saved pasta water.

6. Serve the pasta topped with the caper breadcrumbs and microgreens, with lemon wedges on the side.

NOTE

i   It's best to soak nuts overnight, but a quick soak in boiling water for 15–30 minutes will suffice. You can replace the cashews with toasted sunflower seeds.

YOU WILL NEED

your favourite pasta

FOR THE CASHEW SAUCE

2 tbsp olive oil
2 generous handfuls of cashew nuts, soaked (i)
juice of 1 lemon
2 tbsp caper juice
1 garlic clove
1 tbsp nutritional yeast
250ml/9fl oz/1 cup water

FOR THE CAPER BREADCRUMBS

2 tbsp sunflower seeds
2 tbsp pumpkin seeds
1 tsp dried oregano
zest of 1 lemon
1 tsp paprika
1 tbsp olive oil
2 tbsp capers
3 garlic cloves, sliced
salt and pepper

TO SERVE

microgreens or dill or parsley
lemon wedges

Aubergine/Eggplant Sarmie

with chickpea cutlets, green olives, cashew nut labneh, tomatoes and parsley

serves 2
cooking time: 20 minutes

This is the best breadless sarmie because of its crunchy texture. The fillings are a gentle guide. You can and should go wild with your favourite combinations.

METHOD

1   Preheat the grill/broiler to high and grease an ovenproof dish or baking pan.

2. Coat the aubergine/eggplant in the olive oil. Mix together the flour, nutritional yeast, oregano, salt and pepper and dip the aubergine rounds into the mixture. Place in the prepared dish/pan and grill/broil until golden brown, about 15–20 minutes, turning them over halfway through.

3   Spread the cashew nut labneh on half the aubergine rounds (this will make two sarmies) and stack with two chickpea cutlets, halved cherry tomatoes, parsley and green olives.

4   Finish each sarmie off with another eggplant round and some salt and pepper and chilli sauce (if you're obsessed with chilli like I am).

YOU WILL NEED

1 large aubergine/eggplant, sliced into
   2.5cm/1in rounds
2 tbsp olive oil
2 tbsp flour of your choice
2 tsp nutritional yeast
1 tbsp dried oregano
salt and pepper
Cashew Nut Labneh (see page 81)
4 Chickpea Cutlets (see page 118)
handful of cherry tomatoes, halved
handful of fresh parsley leaves
handful of pitted green olives, sliced
chilli sauce, to serve

La Paz, Baja California Sur, Mexico, shot on a Sony a6500 with a Mitakon Zhongyi fixed 35mm lens

Garlic & Thyme Porcini Mushrooms

with spelt, kale and romesco sauce

serves 2–4
cooking time: 30 minutes

This dish is rustic and simple, and tastes even better if you forage the mushrooms yourself from the forest. Porcinis are heaven. They have a wonderful earthy taste and the most delicious texture. I've paired them with chewy spelt, wilted kale, lots of thyme and a smoky red pepper romesco sauce.

If you can't find fresh porcini, try this recipe with king oyster mushrooms (or any other mushroom) and why not add some texture with the smoky coconut bacon, dukkah or spicy Indian almonds from the Crunchy Toppings section on page 40.

Porcini mushrooms contain a significant amount of protein compared to other vegetables. They are a good source of B vitamins (B2, B3, B5) and minerals such as potassium, copper, selenium, and zinc.

YOU WILL NEED

250g/9oz/1½ cups spelt, soaked
2 tbsp olive oil
220g/7¾oz/3 cups porcini
    mushrooms, sliced (i)
4 garlic cloves, diced
small bunch of fresh thyme sprigs,
    leaves picked
salt and pepper
handful of kale leaves, tough stalks
    removed
250ml/9fl oz/1 cup Smoky Romesco
    Sauce (see page 50)

NOTE

i   If you don't have porcini mushrooms, you can replace this with any other type of mushroom.

METHOD

1   Rinse the spelt until the water runs clear. Place the spelt in a saucepan, cover with water and bring to the boil. Cook for about 20 minutes until it has softened but is still chewy. Drain and rinse.

2   Meanwhile, heat the oil in a pan on a medium heat and add the mushrooms. Fry for 10 minutes until they begin to turn golden, then add the garlic, thyme, salt and pepper.

3   Remove the mushrooms from the pan, then add the kale and sauté until wilted, about 5 minutes.

4   Serve the spelt topped with the fried mushrooms, kale and spoonfuls of romesco sauce.

Tomato & Coconut Bacon Pasta

with a tangy, creamy sundried tomato sauce

serves 2
cooking time: 15 minutes

When I lived in Sri Lanka and Mexico, coconuts were plentiful and coconut bacon was one of my favourite indulgences. It is smoky, salty and crunchy and the perfect addition to any veggie dish. This pasta hits all the right spots with the salty olives, crispy, smoky coconut bacon and creamy, sweet edamame beans. Garden peas would also work beautifully.

METHOD

1   In a food processor or blender, blend the sauce ingredients together until smooth and creamy.

2   Cook the pasta in a pan of boiling salted water according to package directions until al dente. Drain, saving 250ml/9fl oz/1 cup of the pasta water.

3   Heat the sauce through before adding it to the pasta. Mix well and then add the edamame beans, olives and pasta water.

4   Serve with coconut bacon, fresh thyme, good glugs of olive oil and a crisp green salad.

NOTES

i   I love bean, lentil or chickpea pastas for added protein.

ii   Or 400g/14oz can of whole plum tomatoes.

iii   You can use sunflower, hemp, walnuts, almonds, cashews. Ideally soak your choice overnight or quick soak in hot water for 15–30 minutes.

YOU WILL NEED

any pasta of your choice (i)
2 handfuls of steamed edamame/peas
2 handfuls of pitted olives, torn
Smoky Coconut Bacon (see page 40)
a few sprigs of fresh thyme, leaves
    picked
4 handfuls of green salad leaves/
    greens

FOR THE TOMATO SAUCE

6–8 very ripe tomatoes (ii)
6–8 large sundried tomatoes
2 garlic cloves
1 red chilli
2 tbsp olive oil, plus more to serve
handful of fresh basil leaves
handful of nuts/seeds, soaked (iii)
75ml/2½fl oz/⅓ cup water

White Bean Ragu

with parsley and smoky coconut bacon

serves 2
cooking time: 15 minutes

This dish is a beautiful combination of my favourite, simple flavours. The smoky coconut bacon is ideally made using fresh coconuts (the ones that are older and already brown).

I serve this with a lightly warmed raw tomato sauce which is made by simply blending tomatoes, olive oil, chilli and salt. The crunch of the coconut bacon really complements the creamy beans and fresh, tangy tomato sauce.

This works beautifully with the Green Goddess Dressing (see page 61), Turkish Sauce (see page 58), Creamy Mushroom Sauce (see page 75) or the Carrot Top Chimichurri (see page 79).

YOU WILL NEED

1 onion, finely chopped

2 celery stalks, finely chopped

2 small carrots, peeled and finely chopped

2 tbsp olive oil, plus extra to serve

2 garlic cloves, chopped

2 tsp smoked paprika

400g/14oz can of white beans, drained and rinsed

handful of fresh parsley or basil leaves, roughly chopped

2 tomatoes

pinch of dried chilli flakes

salt and pepper

Smoky Coconut Bacon (see page 40)

1 chilli, chopped, to serve

METHOD

1   In a pan over a medium heat, fry the onion, celery and carrots in the olive oil for 5 minutes until golden. Add the garlic and smoked paprika and cook for 2–4 minutes.

2   Add the beans to the pan and cook, stirring regularly, until browned, around 5 minutes.

3   Add the herbs and remove from the heat.

4   Blend the tomatoes with the chilli flakes, salt and a drizzle of olive oil in a food processor until smooth.

5   Serve the beans topped with smoky coconut bacon, the tomato sauce, a few more good glugs of olive oil, salt, pepper and fresh chilli.

Aubergine/Eggplant & Caper Caponata

with garlic green beans, tahini, tzatziki, romesco sauce and pickled radishes

serves 4
cooking time: 30 minutes

This dish is traditionally cooked on the stove and uses loads of olive oil. I love the flavour combinations, but I want the convenience of banging something in the oven and forgetting about it, so I decided to cook the aubergine/eggplant in the oven instead. The result is out of this world.

I love eating like this – a plate of colourful deliciousness, different flavours and textures that send you on a beautiful journey with each mouthful.

METHOD

1   Preheat the oven to 180°C/350°F/Gas 4.

2   Place the aubergine/eggplant in an ovenproof dish, drizzle with olive oil and season with salt and pepper, then bake for 20–30 minutes until golden and soft.

3   Place the green beans in a bowl. Boil the kettle and blanch the green beans in the freshly boiled water for around 2 minutes. Transfer the beans to a frying pan, add the onions, garlic, rosemary, salt and pepper and fry until golden but the beans are still bright green, around 5 minutes. Remove from the heat and toss in the green olives, lemon juice and a drizzle of olive oil.

4   Remove the aubergine from the oven and add the capers, pine nuts and chopped parsley, finishing it off with a few good glugs of olive oil.

5   Serve the caponata and the green beans with tzatziki, tahini, romesco sauce and pickled radishes.

YOU WILL NEED

2 large aubergines/eggplants, cubed
2 tbsp olive oil, plus extra to serve
2 tsp capers
2 handfuls of pine nuts, toasted
2 handfuls of fresh parsley leaves, chopped

FOR THE GREEN BEANS

2 handfuls of green beans
1 onion, chopped
2 garlic cloves, chopped
2 sprigs of fresh rosemary, leaves picked
salt and pepper
handful of pitted green olives, sliced
juice of 1 lemon
1 tbsp olive oil

TO SERVE

Tzatziki (see page 43)
Black Sesame Tahini (see page 76)
Smoky Romesco Sauce (see page 50)
pickled radishes

One Pot, Two Bean Chilli

with mushrooms and guacamole

serves 4
cooking time: 30 minutes

This chilli is beautiful comfort food and delicious when served piled with creamy guacamole and fresh coriander/cilantro. It contains kidney beans and chickpeas/garbanzo beans for a hearty high-protein meal that you can make in around 30 minutes in one pot.

When you have a few cans of chickpeas, tomatoes and beans left in your pantry, this is such a good go-to recipe, packed with so much goodness. Take it to another level by topping with the Dukkah (see page 40), Peanut, Lime & Chilli (see page 41), Coconut Sambal (see page 41) or Salsa Macha (see page 66).

METHOD

1 In a large saucepan on a medium heat, fry the onions, garlic, chilli and spices in the coconut oil for 4–5 minutes until golden. Add the mushrooms and fry for 5 minutes until browned.

2 Add the chopped peppers and courgettes/zucchini and cook until browned, around 5 minutes.

3 Add the chickpeas/garbanzo beans, beans, tomatoes, vegetable stock and your choice of sweetener to reduce the acidity of the tomatoes. Turn down the heat and allow to simmer. The chilli will begin to thicken slowly and should be the consistency of a stew after about 20 minutes of simmering.

4 Meanwhile, mash the avocado with a good pinch of salt, pepper, lemon juice and coriander/cilantro.

5 Serve the chilli piled with the guacamole and more toppings of your choice.

YOU WILL NEED

2 onions, chopped
2 garlic cloves, chopped
I red chilli, chopped
I tsp paprika
I tsp ground coriander
I tbsp coconut oil
handful of mushrooms, sliced
I red pepper, deseeded and cut into
    bite-size chunks
2 large courgettes/zucchini, cut into
    bite-size chunks
400g/14oz can of chickpeas/garbanzo
    beans, drained and rinsed (or
    160g/5²⁄₃oz/I cup dried, soaked
    and cooked)
400g/14oz can of red kidney beans,
    drained and rinsed (or 160g/5²⁄₃oz/I
    cup dried, soaked and cooked)
400g/14oz can of whole peeled
    tomatoes
250ml/9fl oz/I cup vegetable stock
I tsp agave/honey/coconut sugar
2 avocados
Himalayan salt and black pepper
juice of ½ lemon
generous handful fresh coriander/
    cilantro, roughly chopped

JOURNAL ENTRY//
Sometimes we crave movement
because we want to shed layers
and skins and old modes of
thought and ways of being…
and then sometimes all we
want is to nest and root and
grow, comforted by familiar
surroundings, held by stillness
and the beauty of being in one
place for an extended period
of time.

Baja California Sur, Mexico, shot on a Sony a6500 with Mitakon Zhongyi fixed 35mm lens

In this chapter I explore plant-based alternatives to dishes that are traditionally cooked with meat, as well as new creations inspired by my upbringing or travels. For something simple, try the Crumbed Cauliflower Bites on page 191 or the Beetroot/Beet Balls on page 186 and then experiment and get creative with the Nachos of My Dreams on page 231 served with hibiscus flower meat, the jackfruit tostada or vegan sushi with macadamia nuts and shiitake mushrooms.

Plant Proteins

Beetroot/Beet Balls

in a rich tomato and olive sauce with vegan parm

serves 4
cooking time: 30 minutes

When you're craving the old classics like spaghetti and meatballs, do not despair. These beetroot/beet balls will satisfy your craving and more. They are filled with delicious nutritional powerhouses such as hemp seeds and quinoa. Hemp seeds are one of the highest sources of plant-based protein and are considered a complete protein, which means they contain all the essential amino acids. They are also a good source of omega 3 and 6 fats. These beet balls work beautifully in wraps, pitas, salads and Buddha bowls or as a snack dunked into one of the sauces or dips in the Dressed Up chapter.

METHOD

1   Soak the chia seeds in the water for 10 minutes until the mixture forms a gel. Place all the beetroot/beet ball ingredients in a food processor and pulse. The mixture shouldn't be over pulsed, just enough to resemble ground/minced meat. Roll into balls and place in the prepared dish. Chill in the fridge for 15 minutes to firm up.

2   While they're chilling, preheat the oven to 180°C/350°F/Gas 4. Grease an ovenproof dish with a little olive oil.

3   Bake the beetroot balls for around 15 minutes, or until golden.

4   Meanwhile, put all the sauce ingredients (excluding the basil and olives) in a blender and blend until smooth. Pour into a saucepan and add the basil and olives. Bring to the boil and simmer for 10 minutes, adding water (or pasta water) and salt and pepper as needed.

5   Serve on your choice of spaghetti or courgette/zucchini noodles sprinkled with vegan parm.

NOTE

i   I used a combination of hemp seeds and walnuts.

YOU WILL NEED

spaghetti or 4 medium courgettes/
   zucchini, spiralized
Vegan Parm (see page 42)
olive oil, for greasing

FOR THE BEETROOT/
BEET BALLS

2 tbsp chia seeds
75ml/2½fl oz/⅓ cup water
2 beetroots/beets, roughly chopped
1 onion, roughly chopped
4 garlic cloves
thumb-size piece of root ginger
1 tsp ground cumin
1 tsp ground coriander
1 tsp red chilli flakes
2 tbsp dried oregano
200g/7oz/1½ cup cooked quinoa
125g/4½oz/1 cup ground nuts/seeds (i)

FOR THE SAUCE

1 tbsp olive oil
6–8 ripe tomatoes
1 red chilli
4 sundried tomatoes
1 tsp coconut sugar
2–4 garlic cloves
handful of fresh basil leaves, roughly
   chopped
handful of pitted olives, sliced

Here I served the beet balls with a delicious creamy cauliflower mash made simply by puréeing steamed cauliflower with olive oil, salt and pepper. Top with some fresh coriander/cilantro and fennel, smoky coconut bacon, chilli oil and a piece of garlic naan.

Crumbed Cauliflower Bites

with a beet, ginger and lemon sauce

serves 2–4
cooking time: 30 minutes

These crumbed cauliflower bites are a crunchy delight packed with nutrients from hemp, pumpkin and sunflower seeds. Here I serve them on a bed of greens with cashew nut labneh and a beetroot/beet, ginger and lemon sauce. It is beneficial to have a daily serving of foods high in magnesium and B vitamins to assist with hormone regulation, such as legumes, green leafy vegetables, avocados, pistachios and sesame, sunflower and pumpkin seeds.

YOU WILL NEED

handful of hemp seeds
handful of pumpkin seeds
handful of sunflower seeds
salt and pepper
I tsp dried oregano
I tsp paprika
2 tsp chia seeds
75ml/2½fl oz/⅓ cup water
I head of cauliflower, broken into
    florets
2–4 tbsp coconut oil
salt and pepper, to taste
Beetroot/Beet, Ginger & Lemon
    Sauce (see page 53)
Cashew Nut Labneh (see page 81)

METHOD

1   Preheat the oven to 180°C/350°F/Gas 4. Grease and line a baking sheet.

2   Mix the chia seeds with the water and wait until it forms a gel, around 10 minutes.

3   In the meantime, in a food processor, pulse the hemp, pumpkin and sunflower seeds with salt, pepper, oregano and paprika until fine.

4   Coat the cauliflower florets in the chia gel and then roll them in the seed mixture.

5   Bake for 20–30 minutes until golden. Alternatively, in a pan over a medium heat, shallow fry the cauliflower in coconut oil for around 3–5 minutes on each side.

6   Serve sprinkled with salt and pepper, with beetroot/beet, ginger and lemon sauce and cashew nut labneh.

Quick Chickpea Patties

with mushroom sauce, roasted tomatoes, avocado and basil pesto

serves 2–4
cooking time: 20 minutes

These were the first veggie patties I ever made, and I still love them because they are so easy to make, high in protein and really tasty. You can also prepare the patty mixture ahead of time and store it in an airtight container in the fridge for 3–4 days or in the freezer for up to 3 months.

Get creative with different combinations of sauces and toppings for these bad boys.

METHOD

1 Soak the chia seeds in the water until they form a gel, about 10 minutes. Combine the gel with the remaining chickpea patty ingredients in a food processor. Mould the mixture into 4–6 patties.

2 Once the patties have formed, preheat the grill/broiler to high.

3 In a frying pan on a medium heat, fry the patties in olive oil for 3–5 minutes on either side until golden brown and crispy.

4 Put the cherry tomatoes into an ovenproof dish and drizzle with the oil. Grill/broil until slightly blackened and the skins have burst, about 10 minutes.

5 Serve the patties topped with basil pesto, slices of avocado, mushroom sauce and grilled tomatoes.

YOU WILL NEED

handful of cherry tomatoes
2 tbsp olive oil, plus more for frying

FOR THE CHICKPEA PATTIES

1 tbsp chia seeds
75ml/2½fl oz/⅓ cup water
400g/14oz can of chickpeas/garbanzo
    beans, drained and rinsed
½ onion, diced
1 carrot, grated
1 courgette/zucchini, grated
handful of fresh parsley, chopped
1 tsp ground cumin
2 garlic cloves, chopped
2 tbsp nut flour

TO SERVE

Basil Pesto (see page 57)
1 avocado, sliced
Creamy Mushroom Sauce
    (see page 75)

The Kruger National Park, South Africa, shot on a Nikon d90 with a fixed 50mm lens

Lentil Cottage Pie

with tomatoes and turmeric sweet potato mash

serves 4
cooking time: 30 minutes

This is simple to make and high in protein. It reminds me of my childhood, as we always ate cottage pie served with garden peas and salad. It's definitely one of those warming comfort-food dishes that hits all the right spots.

This meat-free version is made with split red lentils, which cook really quickly and are easy to digest, topped with the creamiest turmeric sweet potato mash for the ultimate flavour bomb.

METHOD

1 Rinse the lentils until the water runs clear and place in a saucepan with 1 litre/35fl oz/4 cups of the water. Bring to the boil and simmer until soft, about 20 minutes.

2 Meanwhile, in a pan over a medium heat, sauté the onion and garlic with the paprika and ground coriander in olive oil for 5 minutes until golden. Add the tomatoes, sugar, salt and pepper and simmer for about 20 minutes until thickened.

3 Drain the lentils and add them to the tomato mixture with 250ml/9fl oz/1 cup of water.

4 Cook the sweet potatoes in a pan of boiling water until soft, about 20 minutes. Remove from the heat and drain. Using a hand-held/immersion blender or masher, combine with turmeric, olive oil, salt and pepper until creamy.

5 Spoon the lentils into a serving dish and top with the sweet potato mash and smooth it flat. Serve with garden peas and a salad.

YOU WILL NEED

400g/14oz/2 cups dried red split lentils
1.2 litres/40fl oz/5 cups water
1 onion, finely chopped
4 garlic cloves, finely chopped
1 tsp paprika
1 tsp ground coriander
2 tbsp olive oil
2 x 400g/14oz cans of whole peeled tomatoes
1 tsp coconut sugar
salt and pepper
250ml/9fl oz/1 cup water
4 large sweet potatoes, peeled and cut into chunks
1 tsp ground turmeric
1–2 tbsp olive oil

TO SERVE

4 handfuls of garden peas, cooked
4 handfuls of salad leaves/greens

Seitan Cutlets

with mashed potatoes, grilled/broiled turmeric aubergine/eggplant and gravy

serves 4–6
cooking time: 45 minutes

Seitan was created by Buddhist monks so they could cost-effectively increase their protein intake on a vegetarian diet. It is essentially wheat meat – the protein that remains after you rinse away all the starch from a dough. It has a very chewy texture and you can add any flavour you desire to spice it up.

METHOD

1 To make the seitan, mix the flour with the water until a dough forms. Knead for 3–5 minutes until smooth. Form a well-combined ball and place in a large bowl of cold water.

2 Knead the dough in the bowl until the water is milky, around 3–5 minutes, then replace the water and repeat for about 10 minutes until the water runs clear.

3 Squeeze the dough and press out as much liquid and air as possible. Your dough should be textured, elastic and half the size of your original ball. Use a sharp knife to cut the seitan into 4–6 equal-sized pieces.

4 To make the stock, put all the ingredients into a saucepan and bring to the boil over a high heat. Reduce to a simmer, add the seitan and simmer for 20 minutes. Remove the seitan and save the stock for the gravy.

5 To make the crumbs, pulse all the ingredients in a food processor until fine. Coat the seitan pieces in the crumb mixture.

6 In a frying pan over a medium heat, fry the seitan in coconut oil for 3–5 minutes on each side until golden brown.

7 For the gravy, fry the onion and tomato in coconut oil on a medium heat for 5 minutes until golden. Add the red wine and simmer for 3 minutes until it has cooked away. Add 500ml/17fl oz/2 cups of the stock and simmer for 5–10 minutes until it has cooked down. Finish with a squeeze of lemon juice.

8 Serve with roasted turmeric aubergine/eggplant.

YOU WILL NEED

Roasted Turmeric Aubergine/Eggplant (see page 352)
Coconut oil, for frying

FOR THE SEITAN

750g/1lb 10oz/6¼ cups wholemeal/ whole-wheat flour
500ml/17fl oz/2 cups cold water

FOR THE STOCK

1 litre/35fl oz/4¼ cups water
60ml/2fl oz/¼ cup soy sauce
½ onion, chopped
1 tbsp miso paste
1 tomato, quartered
2 garlic cloves

FOR THE CRUMBS

handful of sunflower seeds
handful of pumpkin seeds
handful of hemp seeds
1 tsp turmeric
1 tsp ground coriander
salt and pepper

FOR THE GRAVY

1 onion, finely chopped
1 tomato, finely chopped
1 tbsp coconut oil
125ml/4fl oz/½ cup glass of red wine
squeeze of lemon juice

The Great Wall of China, shot on a Nikon D90 with a fixed 50mm lens

Cauliflower Steaks & Smoky Chipotle Sauce

with walnut and hemp seed crumble

serves 4
cooking time: 30 minutes

I love these because they hit all the right spots, with the smokiness of the chipotle sauce perfectly balancing the rich and nutty cauliflower steaks.

I would definitely add chilli oil like the Salsa Macha on page 66 and serve with mashed root veggies and greens or oven chips and salad.

METHOD

1 Preheat the oven to 180°C/350°F/Gas 4.

2 Slice the cauliflower into four steaks. It's important to cut from the base of the cauliflower head so that the steaks stay together. Generously brush the pieces of cauliflower in olive oil, making sure they're coated, then place on a baking sheet.

3 Pulse the nuts, seeds and spices in a food processor. Top the cauliflower steaks with the nut crumble, then bake for 20–30 minutes until golden.

4 Combine all the ingredients for the sauce in a blender and blend on high until smooth.

5 Serve the cauliflower steaks with the smoky chipotle sauce.

NOTE

i Other nuts would work well too, such as almonds, pecans, macadamia nuts or Brazil nuts.

YOU WILL NEED

I head of cauliflower
olive oil
2 handfuls of walnuts (i)
handful of hemp seeds
I dried red chilli
I tsp ground ginger
I tsp ground cumin
salt and pepper

FOR THE SMOKY CHIPOTLE SAUCE

3 tbsp tahini
2 tbsp tomato purée/paste
I tbsp canned chipotle chillies
I clove garlic
I tsp smoked paprika
75ml/2½fl oz/⅓ cup water
I tbsp vinegar
salt and pepper

Ground Nut Bolognese

with walnuts, pumpkin seeds and sunflower seeds in a tomato and wild garlic sauce

serves 4
cooking time: 30 minutes

This ground nut blows me away every time. The texture is chewy and crunchy and you make it the same way you're used to making a traditional spaghetti bolognese. You can serve with pasta or courgette/zucchini noodles, as a topping for the Nachos of my Dreams on page 231 or spooned over the Rostis with Sweet Potatoes and Cumin on page 351. I hope you love this one as much as I do.

It is really important to soak your nuts and seeds in order to break down the phytic acid that is hard on digestion. Ideally soak them overnight.

METHOD

1 Begin by pulsing the ground nut ingredients in a food processor until there are no whole nuts or seeds left. Do not over-grind into a powder; you want a texture that resembles ground/minced meat.

2 To make the sauce, in a pan on a medium heat, fry the onion in 1 tablespoon of oil for 4–5 minutes until translucent and then add the garlic. Add extra veggies such as a handful of chopped courgette/zucchini, sliced mushrooms or grated carrots or beetroot/beets.

3 Add the ground nut and stir regularly, browning the mixture for around 5–7 minutes. This part is really important; don't rush the browning as it gives the dish its depth of umami flavour. Add the red wine, if using, and scrape the bottom of the pan to loosen the delicious browned bits.

4 In a blender, add the tomatoes, tomato purée/paste, chilli, the remaining tablespoon of olive oil, coconut sugar, salt and pepper to a blender and combine until creamy.

5 Once the ground nut is browned, add the tomato sauce and 250ml/ 9fl oz/1 cup of water (or pasta water if you are serving with pasta) and simmer on low for 10 minutes until thickened. Add the fresh basil or oregano and wild garlic flowers.

6 Serve with courgette/zucchini noodles or a pasta of your choice.

YOU WILL NEED

pasta, cooked, or 2 courgettes/
zucchini, spiralized and cooked

FOR THE GROUND NUT

2 handfuls of walnuts
handful of pumpkin seeds
handful of sunflower seeds
1 tbsp ground cumin
1 tbsp ground coriander
1 tsp chilli powder
1 tbsp nutritional yeast
salt and pepper

FOR THE SAUCE

1 red onion, diced
2 tbsp olive oil
handful of wild garlic leaves
or 2 garlic cloves
handful of courgette/zucchini,
mushrooms, carrots or beetroot/
beets (optional)
½ glass/75ml/2½fl oz/⅓ cup
red wine (optional)
6 ripe tomatoes/400g/14oz can
of chopped tomatoes
2 tbsp tomato purée/paste
1 chilli, chopped
1 tsp coconut sugar
250ml/9fl oz/1 cup water
handful of fresh basil/oregano leaves
handful of wild garlic flowers
salt and pepper

It is really important to soak and activate your nuts and seeds before consuming in order to break down the phytic acid that is hard on digestion. Ideally soak them overnight.

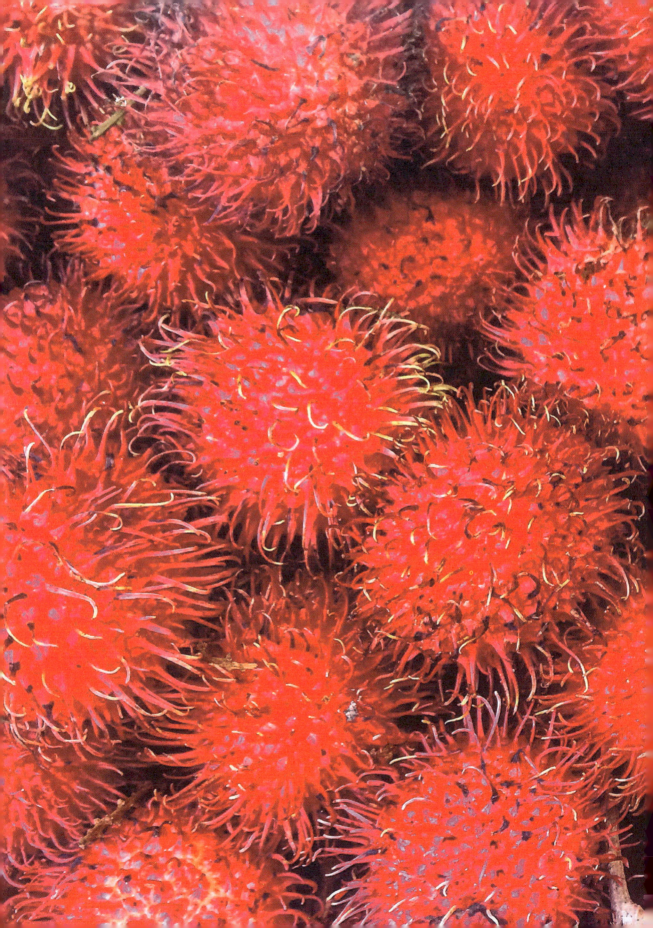

Rambutans, Galle Fort, Sri Lanka, shot on an Iphone 5

Wild Mushroom Stroganoff

with turmeric and cauliflower purée and vegan parm

serves 4
cooking time: 20 minutes

When you crave something rich and creamy, both dark and light, this is the answer to your wildest stroganoff dreams. Mushrooms are sautéed with onions, wine and garlic to create this wonderful stroganoff with the heavenliest, creamiest cauliflower mash that tastes like a rich cheese sauce. Before you cook with mushrooms, place them in the sun for a couple of hours to generate vitamin D, which you can then absorb.

METHOD

1   Place the cauliflower florets in a pot and cover with water. Bring to a simmer and cook until soft, about 10 minutes. Drain and add to a blender with the turmeric, olive oil, salt and pepper. Blend on high until smooth and creamy.

2   In a saucepan on a medium heat, sauté the onions, garlic and coriander seeds in olive oil for 5 minutes until translucent and fragrant. Add the mushrooms and cook until soft and browned, around 10 minutes.

3   Add the wine and cook for 3–4 minutes until the alcohol has evaporated. Turn the heat to low and add the flour. Slowly add water or nut milk and simmer for 5–7 minutes, stirring consistently to create a delicious thick and creamy sauce.

4   Serve the stroganoff ladled over the cauliflower purée and topped with vegan parm.

NOTE

i   Lentil or rice flour works wonderfully.

YOU WILL NEED

FOR THE PURÉE

1 head of cauliflower, broken
     into florets
1 tbsp ground turmeric
2 tbsp olive oil
salt and pepper

FOR THE STROGANOFF

1 onion, chopped
4–6 garlic cloves, chopped
1 tsp coriander seeds, crushed
1 tbsp olive oil
4 handfuls of mushrooms, sliced
     (your choice)
½ glass/75ml/2½fl oz/⅓ cup wine
     (red or white)
1 tbsp flour (i)
100ml/3⅓fl oz/½ cup nut milk,
     plus extra for a looser consistency
     if desired
Vegan Parm (see page 42),
     to serve

Leaf Tacos

with crispy hibiscus flowers and mint tahini

serves 2
cooking time: 15 minutes

I recently discovered that I was anaemic and needed to increase my iron intake. Did you know that hibiscus is incredibly high in iron? So much so that a cup of hibiscus tea a day is equal to your recommended daily allowance of iron. Once you've used these dried flowers to make tea, they make the perfect meat substitute because of their chewy texture.

If you can't get hold of hibiscus, try the leaf tacos with pieces of my Falafel Schnitzels (see page 236), Beetroot/Beet Balls (see page 186), Ground Nut Bolognese (see page 204) or Seitan Cutlets (see page 198). Serve with turmeric mayo, Salsa Macha (see page 66) and Green Goddess Dressing (see page 61).

METHOD

1   Rinse the hibiscus flowers a couple of times. Place in a saucepan, cover with water and bring to the boil over a medium heat. Boil for 5 minutes, then remove from the heat and allow to sit for 5 minutes.

2   Fry the cumin in olive oil for 20–30 seconds until fragrant. Add the tomato purée/paste, mustard, agave, salt and pepper and stir.

3   Drain the hibiscus flowers, saving the infused water to drink as tea. I love it iced with lemon, mint and agave.

4   Pat the flowers dry before adding them to the pan. Toss in the pan and sauté on high until slightly browned and crispy, around 5–7 minutes. Add the vinegar and turn off the heat.

5   Combine the tahini ingredients in a blender until smooth, adding water until you've reached your desired consistency, not too runny but creamy and smooth to drizzle over the tacos.

6   To serve, fill cos/romaine lettuce leaves with the hibiscus meat, red pepper slices, avocado chunks and coriander/cilantro, then drizzle with the mint tahini.

YOU WILL NEED

FOR THE SMOKY HIBISCUS FLOWER MEAT
2 handfuls of dried hibiscus flowers
2 tsp ground cumin
2 tbsp olive oil
2 tbsp tomato purée/paste
1 tsp mustard
1 tsp agave/coconut sugar
salt and pepper
1 tbsp red wine vinegar

FOR THE MINT TAHINI
handful of fresh mint
2 tbsp tahini
1–2 tbsp fresh lime/lemon juice
1 tsp agave
1 garlic clove

TO SERVE
cos/romaine lettuce leaves
red pepper slices
avocado chunks
fresh coriander/cilantro

210

Baja California Sur, Mexico, shot on a Pentax K1000 with a fixed 35mm lens

Veggie Burgers

with mushrooms, black beans, wild rice and kale

makes around 8–10 patties
cooking time: 30 minutes

I have been striving for the ultimate texture and taste of a veggie burger and have come up with a simple way of creating some mouth-watering combinations. Try sage, oregano, brown lentil and onion; beetroot/beet, mint and almond; black bean, thyme and mushroom; chickpea/garbanzo bean, cumin and red pepper; butter bean, sundried tomatoes and basil; or green peas, mint and pistachio. This recipe is the perfect balance of ingredients for a nutritious veggie burger that's full of protein and high in fibre.

METHOD

1   Soak the chia seeds in the water until they form a gel, about 10 minutes.

2   Meanwhile, combine all your chosen burger ingredients in a food processor and pulse until chunky. Add the chia egg to the food processor and blend to combine.

3   Mould the mixture into 8–10 patties and place in the freezer or fridge for at least 15 minutes to firm up.

4   Grill on the barbeque, fry in a pan on medium-high heat for 4–6 minutes each side or grill/broil in the oven.

5   Serve with your favourite sauces.

NOTES

i   Or 150g/5¼oz/⅔ cups dried, soaked and cooked.

ii   Such as buckwheat, spelt, quinoa, wild rice, millet, amaranth, couscous.

iii   Different combinations work beautifully: you can try kale, mushrooms, onions, carrots, leeks, broccoli, celery, sweet potato, peppers, sundried tomatoes or olives.

iv   Sage, thyme, rosemary, mint and basil are all good options.

v   Choose from cumin, black pepper, ground coriander, chilli, paprika, cayenne and turmeric.

vi   I'd recommend sunflower, pumpkin, sesame seeds or hemp hearts.

YOU WILL NEED

1 tbsp chia seeds
75ml/2½fl oz/⅓ cup water

FOR THE BURGERS

400g/14oz can of black beans, lentils or chickpeas/garbanzo beans, drained and rinsed (i)
200g/7oz/2 cups high-protein cooked grains (ii)
2 onions, roughly chopped
2 handfuls of vegetables (iii)
handful of fresh herbs (iv)
1 tbsp each of garlic, root ginger and chilli (optional)
a few pinches of different spices (v)
2 tbsp flour (oat, almond, chickpea)
handful of nuts and seeds (vi)
salt and pepper

Aubergine/Eggplant Schnitzel

crispy aubergine/eggplant coated in seeds with raw tomato chilli sauce

serves 2
cooking time: 20 minutes

This crumbed aubergine/eggplant is so moreish, and the fresh, sharp tomato sauce complements it perfectly. I love serving this with something creamy like mashed potato or polenta/cornmeal and a pile of greens such as My Take on the Classic Caesar on page 246.

A delicious way to make use of sourdough bread crusts is to add them to your food processor and pulse until fine. You can use these breadcrumbs instead of the nuts and seeds in this recipe.

Did you know that the skin of the aubergine is rich in antioxidants, fibre, potassium and magnesium? Leave the skin on so you don't miss out on all these health benefits.

METHOD

1 Preheat the grill/broiler to high.

2 Cut the aubergine/eggplant lengthways into 1cm/½in slices and coat in olive oil.

3 Blitz the rest of the schnitzel ingredients in a food processor until fine. Coat the aubergine slices in the crumb mixture then place on a baking sheet. Grill/broil for 10 minutes on each side.

4 In a blender, combine the tomato sauce ingredients until smooth.

5 Serve the schnitzels with the raw tomato sauce.

YOU WILL NEED

1 large aubergine/eggplant
olive oil
handful of pumpkin/sunflower seeds
handful of nuts
2 tbsp oat flour/ground almonds/
    coconut flour
1 tsp dried oregano
1 tsp red chilli flakes
1 tsp smoked paprika
1 tsp ground cumin
salt and pepper
2–4 tbsp avocado/olive/hemp oil

FOR THE TOMATO CHILLI SAUCE

2 ripe tomatoes
1 garlic clove
1 red chilli
1 tbsp olive oil

The wound is the place
where the light enters you.

Rumi

Noordhoek Beach, Cape Town, shot on a Panasonic GH4 with a Canon fixed 50mm lens

Herby Oat & Sweet Potato Balls

with broccoli and seeds

makes around 20 balls
cooking time: 30 minutes

The texture of these oat balls is unbelievably good: crispy on the outside and chewy on the inside. They are full of flavour and are baked, not fried.

They are delicious in pita pockets with hummus and grilled veggies or served with salad, sauces and some naan bread. Throw them in a wrap or toss them in homemade tomato sauce and serve them with veggies. The options are endless.

METHOD

1 Preheat the oven to 180°C/350°F/Gas 4 and grease a baking dish with a little olive oil.

2 Mix the chia seeds with the water and set aside for 10 minutes until a gel has formed.

3 Meanwhile, pulse half of the oats with the walnuts and sunflower seeds in a food processor. Do not over pulse – you want some chunkier pieces in there for texture. Tip into a bowl and add the rest of the ingredients. Add the chia gel once it is ready and combine.

4 Form the mixture into balls and place in the prepared baking dish. Bake until golden brown, around 30 minutes.

5 Serve with your favourite sides and toppings.

NOTES

i Or 1 tsp onion powder.

ii Or ½ tsp garlic powder.

YOU WILL NEED

2 tbsp chia seeds

75ml/2½fl oz/⅓ cup water

100g/3½oz/1¼ cups rolled oats

90g/3¼oz/1 cup ground walnuts

75g/2⅔oz/½ cup sunflower seeds

125ml/4fl oz/½ cup olive oil

1 small sweet potato, grated

90g/3¼oz/1 cup broccoli, finely chopped

1 onion, finely chopped (i)

2 garlic cloves, finely chopped (ii)

2 tsp dried oregano

2 tsp ground coriander

1 tsp salt

black pepper

Jackfruit Tostada

serves 4
cooking time: 40 minutes

I ate jackfruit for the first time in Sri Lanka. Jackfruit is the largest tree fruit in the world, a massive bright-green fruit with a rough, spiky exterior. It has become popular in plant-based diets, as it has a texture comparable to shredded meat. The unripe jackfruit is used as a vegetable in Sri Lankan cooking, and it is delicious cooked in a curry. Jackfruit is a superfood with anti-aging and antioxidant properties and high levels of vitamins A and C and magnesium. You could try substituting mushrooms for jackfruit in my Mushroom Masala recipe on page 313.

I like to serve this with avocado, tomato salsa, jalapeños and lime but you can choose any of your favourite toppings.

METHOD

1   To make the tostadas, place the buckwheat flour and salt in a bowl and make a well in the centre. Slowly add the water and oil. Mix with a wooden spoon and and knead with your hands for 1–2 minutes until smooth. If the dough is sticky, add a bit more flour. Cover the dough and place in the fridge for 30 minutes.

2   Meanwhile, in a pan on a medium heat, fry the spices in the coconut oil until fragrant, around 1 minute. Add the onion and garlic and fry until translucent, around 5 minutes. Add the jackfruit and sauté until browned, around 5 minutes. At this point, mix in the BBQ sauce (if using) salt, pepper and a squeeze of lime or lemon juice.

3   Liberally flour your surface, divide the dough into balls roughly the size of a golf ball (about 10–12) and and use a rolling pin to roll the tortillas out into circular shapes – be gentle as the dough is quite delicate.

4   Heat 2 tablespoons of the coconut oil in a frying pan over medium–high heat. Once hot, carefully add the tortillas and fry for 1–2 minutes on each side until crispy and golden brown. Drain on paper towels.

5   Serve the shredded barbecue jackfruit on the homemade buckwheat tostadas with your favourite toppings.

YOU WILL NEED

1 tsp ground cumin
1 tsp ground coriander
1 tsp red chilli flakes
1 tbsp coconut oil, plus extra for frying
1 red onion, finely chopped
2 garlic cloves, finely chopped
400g/14oz can of jackfruit, drained
4 tbsp BBQ sauce (see page 62) (optional)
salt and pepper
squeeze of lime/lemon juice

FOR THE BUCKWHEAT TOSTADA (i)

250g/9oz/2 cups buckwheat flour
pinch of salt
130ml/4½fl oz/½ cup water
2 tbsp olive oil

NOTE

i   If you don't feel like making the tostada from scratch, simply fry tortillas in the same way.

Rio Celeste, Costa Rica, shot on a Pentax K1000 with a fixed 35mm lens

Pulled BBQ Sweet Potato

with roasted turmeric aubergine/eggplant

serves 4
cooking time: 20 minutes

*When you're craving something smoky, sticky and chewy, look no further. This
pulled sweet potato is delicious in sarmies or wraps or on its own with sides.*

METHOD

1 Heat the olive oil in a frying pan on a medium heat and when hot, throw
in the coriander seeds, cooking for 1–2 minutes until fragrant. Add the
onion and garlic and sauté for 5 minutes until golden brown.

2 Squeeze the grated potato to drain the liquid, then add to the pan.
Stir-fry until golden brown, around 7 minutes.

3 Add the BBQ sauce and simmer for a further 5–10 minutes until
the sauce has reduced.

4 Serve with the roasted aubergine/eggplant, some lime wedges and
any other favourite sides.

YOU WILL NEED

2 tbsp olive oil

1 tbsp coriander seeds, crushed

1 large onion, finely chopped

2 garlic cloves, diced

4 large sweet potatoes, peeled and
grated

250ml/9fl oz/1 cup BBQ sauce
(see page 62)

Roasted Turmeric Aubergine/Eggplant
(see page 352) (i)

lime wedges, to serve

NOTE

i You can cut the roasted aubergine/
eggplant into any shape – here I've
created wedges instead of the bite-
size chunks on page 352.

Lentil Moussaka Stacks

with cashew cream cheese sauce

serves 2–4
cooking time: 45 minutes

This meal is quite simple and a celebration for the taste buds. You could elevate this dish further by adding one of the Crunchy Toppings (see pages 40–43) like Vegan Parm, Dukkah or the Mediterranean Dream.

METHOD

1 Preheat the oven to 180°C/350°F/Gas 4 and grease a muffin or baking pan.

2 In a saucepan on a medium heat, sauté the onion and garlic in oil with the cumin until translucent, about 5 minutes. Add the blended tomatoes and simmer for 5 minutes. Add the sugar, lentils and water and cook for 5 minutes.

3 Meanwhile, in a blender, combine the soaked cashews with the mustard, lemon juice, nutritional yeast and water. The sauce should be creamy but pourable, so add more water as needed.

4 In the greased pan, layer the aubergine/eggplant first, then spoon the lentils on top, finishing with a generous layer of the cashew cream cheese sauce (save some for serving).

5 Sprinkle the seeds over the top with a drizzle of olive oil, then bake for 30 minutes.

6 Serve with more cashew cheese sauce over the top and sprinkle with fresh herbs. These are delicious with a simple crunchy green salad.

NOTES

i   Such as oregano, basil or thyme.

ii Sunflower seeds will work perfectly too.

YOU WILL NEED

1 red onion, finely chopped

4 garlic cloves, finely chopped

2 tbsp olive/coconut/avocado oil, plus more for drizzling

1 tsp ground cumin

2 tomatoes, blended

1 tsp coconut sugar

400g/14oz can of lentils, drained and rinsed

250ml/9fl oz/1 cup water

2 large aubergines/eggplants, thinly sliced into rounds

handful of fresh herbs (i)

handful of sunflower or sesame seeds

2 handfuls of green salad leaves/ greens, to serve

FOR THE CASHEW CHEESE SAUCE

150g/5¼oz/1 cup cashew nuts, soaked in water overnight (or quick soak for 15–30 minutes in boiling water) (ii)

1 tsp mustard

2 tbsp lemon juice

2 tbsp nutritional yeast

125ml/4fl oz/½ cup water (or more as needed)

Nachos of My Dreams

with smoky hibiscus flowers, spicy tomato salsa, green olive tahini cream and walnut cheese

serves 4
cooking time: 10 minutes

These nachos are what dreams are made of. Dried hibiscus flowers are sold online or at your nearest health shop. However, if you can't find them, you can make these nachos with the Ground Nut Bolognese on page 204.

METHOD

1   Rinse the hibiscus flowers a couple of times, then place them in a saucepan on a medium heat and cover with water. Boil for 5 minutes. Remove from the heat and allow to infuse for 5 minutes.

2   To make the smoky hibiscus flower meat, fry the cumin in olive oil in a pan on a medium heat for 30 seconds. Add the tomato purée/paste, mustard, agave, salt and pepper and stir. Drain the hibiscus flowers, saving the infused water. Pat them dry and add to the pan. Sauté on high until slightly browned, about 5–7 minutes. Add the vinegar and remove from the heat.

3   In a food processor, pulse all the tomato salsa ingredients until slightly chunky. For a deeper flavour, you can roast the tomatoes, garlic, ginger and peppers for 30 minutes before adding to the food processor.

4   Pulse the walnut cheese ingredients in a food processor once or twice for a chunky texture. Squeeze lime juice all over the avocado and sprinkle with salt.

5   Lay the tortilla chips out on a large serving plate. Spread the hibiscus flower meat evenly over the chips, then the avocado pieces, dollops of the tomato salsa, lashings of the tahini cream and a generous sprinkle of the walnut cheese. Serve with lime wedges.

NOTES

i   You could swap these for sunflower seeds, almonds or cashews. If you don't have time for an overnight soak, do a quick soak for 15–30 minutes in boiling water.

ii   Or 400g/14oz can of chopped tomatoes.

YOU WILL NEED

fresh limes
1 ripe avocado, cut into chunks
250g/9oz tortilla chips
Green Olive Tahini Cream
   (see page 232)

FOR THE SMOKY HIBISCUS FLOWER MEAT

2 handfuls of dried hibiscus flowers
2 tsp dried cumin
2 tbsp olive oil
2 tbsp tomato purée/paste
1 tsp mustard
1 tsp agave/coconut sugar
sea salt and pepper
1 tbsp red wine vinegar

FOR THE SPICY TOMATO SALSA

4 tomatoes, diced (ii)
4 garlic cloves
½ thumb-sized piece of root ginger
2 small poblano peppers
1 tbsp tomato purée/paste
1 tbsp tahini
juice of 1 lime
salt and pepper

FOR THE WALNUT CHEESE

handful of walnuts, soaked overnight (i)
1 garlic clove
2 tbsp nutritional yeast
1 tsp dried oregano
pinch of salt
black pepper

Green Olive Tahini Cream

Note: you can buy store-bought tahini for this recipe, but I've included how to make you're own as I think it's a lovely addition.

145g/5oz/1 cup sesame seeds
2 tbsp olive oil
juice of ½ a lemon
salt and pepper
3 tbsp water, plus more as needed
handful of sliced green olives
1 tsp agave

If you're making your own tahini, in a pan, dry toast the sesame seeds on medium until lightly browned. Pulse in a food processor until fine. Slowly add the olive oil and blend until smooth and creamy, scraping down the sides if neccessary. Transfer 2 tablespoons of the tahini into a bowl and add the lemon juice, salt and pepper. Slowly add the water until it forms a lovely smooth cream.

Add the sliced olives, more water and another squeeze of lemon, plus a drizzle of something sweet.

These nachos are heaven on a plate. The smoky hibiscus flowers, creamy Green Olive Tahini Cream, avocado chunks and walnut cheese are something special together on a corn chip dunked in some homemade tomato salsa.

Playa Las Palmas, Baja California Sur, Mexico, shot on a Sony a6500 with a Mitakon Zhongyi fixed 35mm lens

Falafel Schnitzels

with cashew cheese sauce

serves 4
cooking time: 15 minutes

These schnitzels are made in the exact same way that traditional falafels are. First you soak your dried chickpeas/garbanzo beans overnight, then you blend them up with herbs like parsley, mint and coriander/cilantro. You can form the mixture into balls (for traditional falafels), patties or schnitzels and bake or fry. If making falafel balls, roll in a mixture of black and white sesame seeds before baking or frying.

METHOD

1   Combine all the ingredients except the sauerkraut and the Cheesiest "No-cheese" sauce in a food processor until a smooth paste has formed.

2   Shape the mixture into balls, patties or schnitzels (around 8–16 depending on size) and chill in the fridge for 15–30 minutes.

3   In a frying pan on a medium heat, shallow fry the falafel in coconut or olive oil until golden brown and crispy, around 3 minutes each side for falafel balls and 6 minutes each side for schnitzels.

4   You can alternatively brown both sides and then place them in the oven to bake for 20 minutes at 180°C/350°F/Gas 4, flipping them halfway through.

5   Serve with sauerkraut and cheese sauce.

YOU WILL NEED

350g/12oz/2 cups dried chickpeas/
    garbanzo beans, soaked overnight
2 garlic cloves
1 tsp baking powder
1 onion, chopped
1 tbsp chickpea flour
handful of fresh parsley leaves
handful of fresh mint leaves
handful of fresh coriander/cilantro
    leaves
1 tbsp ground cumin
1 tbsp ground coriander
salt and pepper
2–4 tbsp coconut or olive oil
Sauerkraut (see page 36)
Cheesiest "No-Cheese" Sauce
    (see page 49)

The Ultimate Vegan Sushi

with macadamia nuts, shiitake mushrooms, microgreens and crispy onions

serves 4–6
cooking time: 45 minutes

I first ate vegan sushi in California, and I was sceptical. Sushi is all about amazing fresh fish, right? But the crunchy macadamia nuts and soft shiitake with creamy avocado, crispy onions and cucumber, salty nori and creamy coriander/cilantro dressing made this become a meal I crave all the time.

I have not included quantities as this is a gentle guide for you to get creative with your vegan sushi rolls. Generally, you'll want about 125g/4½oz/½ cup of cooked rice per person.

METHOD

1 Make the rice according to the packet directions. Add rice wine vinegar, mirin and salt while the rice is still warm, stirring through with a wooden spoon.

2 In a frying pan on a medium heat, sauté the mushrooms in soy sauce and sesame oil for about 5–8 minutes until browned.

3 To make the California rolls, place cling film/plastic wrap over your bamboo rolling mat. Place a sheet of nori on top, then press the rice down firmly across the whole surface of the nori. Layer the fillings along the length of the rice in a line.

4 Roll up your sushi rolls tightly so the fillings don't fall out. You can get creative with your toppings. Slithers of ginger or avocado on top of the roll, with crunchy onions and coconut pieces, work amazingly.

6 Sprinkle with microgreens and sesame seeds and serve with drizzles of sesame oil and ponzu.

7 In a blender, combine all the sauce ingredients together until smooth and creamy. Use as a dip or drizzle over some of your rolls.

YOU WILL NEED

sushi rice, rinsed and drained

4 tbsp rice vinegar

1 tbsp mirin

½ tsp salt for every 750g/13oz/3 cups cooked rice

shiitake mushrooms

soy sauce

sesame oil

nori sheets

macadamia nuts, halved

cucumber, cut into matchsticks

avocado, sliced

crispy fried onions

carrots, peeled and sliced

spring onions/scallions, chopped

wasabi

root ginger, thinly sliced

coconut chips

microgreens

black and white sesame seeds

ponzu sauce

FOR THE DRESSING

handful of fresh coriander/cilantro

handful of sunflower seeds, soaked

2 tbsp lemon juice

about 75ml/2½fl oz/⅓ cup water

1 garlic clove

Prince Alfred Pass, South Africa, shot on a Sony a6500 with a Mitakon Zhongyi fixed 35mm lens

Lake Atitlán, Guatemala, shot on an Iphone 5

To the mind that is still
The whole universe
surrenders

Lao Tzu,
The *Tao Te Ching*

Salads have the potential to be boring, but they can also be wonderfully colourful and scrumptious with textures and dressings that transform them into a meal on their own. In this chapter, I explore adding colourful edible flowers, a variety of grains, roasted veggies and crunchy toppings to salads. Try the Vietnamese Rice Paper Rolls on page 256 or the three hummus plates on pages 279–285 for something a little different.

Fresh Foliage

My Take on a Classic Caesar

with toasted sunflower seeds, avocado, green olives and a lemony, caper dressing

serves 2
cooking time: 15 minutes

Crunchy cos/romaine lettuce, salty green olives, toasted sunflower seeds and the creamiest, garlickiest lemony dressing you ever did taste. You won't even miss the anchovies because the capers are so wonderfully salty and sour. Also, cashews are expensive, so sunflower seeds are the sun's answer to this dressing of dreams.

METHOD

1 Arrange the cos/romaine lettuce leaves on a salad platter and top with chunks of avocado, spring onions/scallions and green olives.

2 Toast the sunflower seeds in a dry pan on a medium heat for 5 minutes until golden brown.

3 Combine the dressing ingredients in a blender until creamy.

4 Pour the dressing over the salad and top with more capers and toasted sunflower seeds.

YOU WILL NEED

1 large head of cos/romaine lettuce
1 avocado, cut into chunks
2 spring onions/scallions, sliced
handful of pitted green olives, sliced
handful of sunflower seeds (i)
2 tbsp capers

FOR THE DRESSING

handful of cashew nuts/sunflower
    seeds, soaked overnight or quick
    soaked in boiling water for 30
    minutes
juice of ½ lemon/lime
2 tbsp olive oil
1 tbsp capers
1 tbsp caper juice
1 tsp agave/honey/coconut nectar
75ml/2½fl oz/⅓ cup water

NOTE

i   Toast the seeds in a dry pan over a
    medium heat for a couple of minutes
    until browned.

Roasted Butternut & Buckwheat Salad

with Kalamata olives and green goddess dressing

serves 4
cooking time: 30 mins

Buckwheat is a goddess when it comes to nutrients. Commonly mistaken for a kind of wheat, buckwheat is actually a plant that produces tiny steel-cut-oat-like seeds. These seeds contain antioxidants and highly digestible protein and are gluten free. Use this incredible plant in place of oats in salads, muesli, porridge and soups. You could also try this salad with the Smoky Romesco Sauce on page 50, the Turkish Sauce on page 58 and the Ginger & Turmeric Sauce on page 46.

I like to finish this off with something crunchy like toasted sunflower or pumpkin seeds, toasted nuts or crispy onions.

METHOD

1   Preheat the oven to 200°C/400°F/Gas 6.

2   Rinse the buckwheat in a colander until the water runs clear. Place the buckwheat and water in a saucepan over a high heat. Put the lid on, bring to the boil, remove the lid and cook until all the water has been absorbed, around 20 minutes. Remove from the heat and put the lid on to steam.

3   In the meantime, toss the butternut chunks in a roasting pan with the olive oil, whole garlic cloves and salt and pepper. Roast for 25–30 minutes, turning halfway through.

4   To assemble, start by rinsing the buckwheat and then layering it in a dish as the base. Top with the butternut squash and cucumber chunks, olives, basil leaves and pomegranate.

5   Serve with generous lashings of the green goddess dressing and topped with wild garlic flowers.

YOU WILL NEED

180g/6⅓oz/1 cup buckwheat, dehulled

500ml/17fl oz/2 cups water

140g/5oz/1 cup butternut squash, cut into chunks (i)

1 tsp olive oil

4 garlic cloves

salt and pepper

¼ cucumber, cubed

handful of pitted Kalamata olives

handful of fresh basil leaves

2 tbsp pomegranate seeds

125ml/4fl oz/½ cup Green Goddess Dressing (see page 61) (ii)

wild garlic flowers, to serve

NOTE

i   This salad would work with any roasted squash you have available to you.

ii Add the garlic you roast with the butternut to the green goddess dressing when you make it.

Crunchy Cabbage Salad

with beetroot/beets, toasted walnuts, olives and a citrus ginger dressing

serves 4–6
prep time: 20 minutes

This salad reminds me of hot summer days, slow lunches and good friends. It is simple, crunchy and salty and has a zingy citrus kick in the dressing. I love everything about each mouthful.

I haven't given exact quantities or measurements for this recipe – with a salad like this it is good to be intuitive. This salad works incredibly well with the Cashew Nut Labneh on page 81.

METHOD

1   Place all the salad ingredients in a large bowl except the walnuts and cheese.

2   Combine the dressing ingredients by shaking them together in a glass jar.

3   Pour the dressing over the salad and top with turmeric dusting, the toasted nuts and cheese and serve.

NOTES

i   Please ensure that the marigold you are using is edible and not toxic.

YOU WILL NEED

various seasonal greens, torn/
chopped
edible flowers like nasturtiums,
marigolds or pansies (i)
½ small cabbage, shredded/grated
1 raw beetroot/beet, peeled and
spiralized
Kalamata olives, pitted and chopped
cucumber, sliced
fennel leaves
walnuts, chopped and toasted
Cashew Nut Labneh (see page 81)

FOR THE DRESSING

¼ tsp ground turmeric, plus a couple
of pinches to serve
juice and zest of 1 lemon
4 tbsp olive oil
1 tsp honey/agave/maple syrup
squeeze or two of grapefruit juice
1 tsp grated root ginger

Bowls of Goodness

with coconut mint chutney, sauerkraut, pickled beetroot/beets and salsa macha

serves 4
cooking time: 20 minutes

This is pretty much my favourite way to eat. A little bit of everything in one bowl, something tangy, sweet, sour and pickled. I created this bowl as a visual example of what you can do to add depth and flavour to your meals. I find that having things like dips, dressings, sauces, pickles and ferments prepared and stored in the fridge is very helpful when putting together a delicious bowl of goodness in no time at all.

METHOD

1 For the coconut chutney, pulse the ingredients in a food processor until well combined but still slightly chunky, adding water to loosen the mixture.

2 For the pickled beetroot/beets, place all the ingredients in a jar with a lid and leave for an hour (for a quick pickle) or a couple of days for a more distinct flavour.

3 To assemble, spoon the lentils, sauerkraut, salsa macha, diced cucumber, fresh mint leaves and pickled beetroot into a bowl. You can go a step further and add the roasted aubergine/eggplant and some finely crushed peanuts.

4 This bowl food is a delicious way to eat and combine a few of your favourite dishes and sauces in one mind-blowing, flavour exploding meal.

YOU WILL NEED

Dhal Tadka (see page 298)
Sauerkraut (see page 36)
Salsa Macha (see page 66)
I cucumber, finely chopped
2 handfuls of fresh mint leaves
Roasted Turmeric Aubergine/Eggplant (see page 352) (optional)
handful of unsalted peanuts, finely crushed and toasted (optional)

FOR THE COCONUT MINT CHUTNEY

80g/2¾oz/I cup desiccated/dried shredded coconut
juice of I small lemon/lime
2 handfuls of fresh corainder/cilantro leaves
I tsp coconut sugar
I tsp grated root ginger
I green chilli, deseeded

FOR THE BEETROOT/BEETS

4 beetroot/beets, julienned or grated
4–6 cloves
I tsp coriander seeds
couple of bay leaves
2 tbsp vinegar
250ml/9fl oz/I cup water
I tsp salt

Gifts from my garden at home in South Africa, shot on
a Sony a6500 with a Mitakon Zhongyi fixed 35mm lens

Vietnamese Rice Paper Rolls

with crunchy veg, edible flowers and peanut sauce

prep time: 15 minutes

I have always adored rice paper rolls because of their fragrant and fresh nature. These are even more appealing with the cheeky addition of edible flowers, which send the senses on a journey of colours that make you feel like you are eating a rainbow. I haven't included quantities as this is a great recipe to prepare for big gatherings of friends (and for everyone to make together).

METHOD

1   In a frying pan on a medium heat, sauté the mushrooms, ginger, chilli and garlic in the coconut oil for about 5 minutes. Add a drizzle of sesame oil and soy sauce, a squeeze of lime juice and salt and pepper.

2   Pour warm water into a shallow dish and soak the rice papers one at a time (until they soften). They become soft and pasta-like, so work quickly when wrapping the crunchy stuffing.

3   Begin with some flower petals and basil leaves down the centre of the rice paper. Place cucumber, carrot, red cabbage, a couple of mushrooms, some bits of sliced ginger, bean sprouts and spring onion/scallions in the middle of the rice paper. Roll over once, tuck both ends in and continue rolling. The rice paper becomes sticky and easy to roll. Repeat with the rest of the rice papers and fillings

4   Combine all the peanut dipping sauce ingredients in a blender on high until creamy. Serve the rice paper rolls with the peanut dipping sauce on the side

NOTE

i   Prepare quantities according to the amount of people you are feeding.

YOU WILL NEED

200g/7oz/2 cups mushrooms, sliced, or tempeh/tofu/aubergine/eggplant cubes

I tsp grated root ginger, plus extra sliced ginger to serve

I chilli, diced

I tsp grated garlic

I tsp coconut oil

sesame oil

light soy sauce

squeeze of lime juice

salt and pepper, to taste

Vietnamese rice paper sheets (i)

edible flowers

basil leaves

cucumber, cut into strips

carrots, cut into strips

red cabbage, sliced

bean sprouts

spring onions/scallions, chopped

peanuts

FOR THE PEANUT DIPPING SAUCE

2 tbsp light soy sauce

2 tbsp lime juice

I chilli, chopped

I tsp chopped root ginger

I tsp coconut sugar/agave

handful of peanuts, toasted and crushed

Vashisht, Himachal Pradesh, India, shot on a Panasonic GH4 with a fixed 50mm lens

Sweet Potato Wedges & Sprout Salad

with garlic and lemon aioli

serves 2
cooking time: 25 minutes

Sweet potato wedges add a sticky, crunchy element to this wholesome high-protein salad that's filled with fresh veggies. This aioli has become a favourite of mine and reminds me of a vegan mayo, but is even more delicious.

METHOD

1   Preheat the oven to 180°C/350°F/Gas 4.

2   Place the sweet potato wedges and garlic cloves for the aioli in an ovenproof dish, drizzle with olive oil and sprinkle with salt, pepper and cumin seeds. Roast until golden brown, around 25 minutes.

3   Meanwhile, toast the sunflower seeds in a dry pan on a medium heat for 5 minutes until golden brown. Place all the salad ingredients in a bowl and toss together.

4   Combine all the ingredients for the aioli in a blender (plus the garlic you roasted with the sweet potatoes) until smooth and creamy, adding more water until you have reached a consistency that resembles aioli or mayonnaise.

5   Serve the sweet potato wedges over the salad topped with the aioli and a lemon wedge.

NOTES

i   Peel before blending.

ii   Quick soak the cashews in boiling water for 15–30 minutes.

YOU WILL NEED

2 sweet potatoes, cut into wedges

2 tbsp olive oil

salt and pepper

2 tsp cumin seeds

FOR THE SPROUT SALAD

handful of sunflower seeds

1 green pepper, deseeded and cut into
    chunks

½ cucumber, cut into bite-size chunks

handful of fresh flat-leaf parsley

handful of sprouts (I used lentil and
    chickpea/garbanzo beans)

handful of pitted Kalamata olives

handful of feta cheese cubes

lemon wedges, to serve

FOR THE LEMON AND GARLIC AIOLI

2–6 garlic cloves, whole and skin on
    (i)

handful of cashew nuts, soaked
    overnight (ii)

juice of 1 lemon/lime

1 tsp mustard

1 tbsp olive oil

75ml/2½fl oz/⅓ cup water

Roasted Cauliflower & Mint Salad

serves 2–4
cooking time: 15–20 minutes

I love this warm salad because it takes very little effort to throw together and is lovely to eat when the weather is cooler but you still want something light and nourishing. This crunchy, spicy roasted cauliflower can be served with the Toasted Coriander Dressing on page 45, the Turkish Sauce on page 58, the Green Goddess Dressing on page 61, the Salsa Macha on page 66 or the Carrot Top Chimichurri on page 79.

METHOD

1   Preheat the oven to 180°C/350°F/Gas 4.

2   Place all the ingredients except the feta and mint in a baking pan, toss gently until well combined, then bake until golden brown, about 15–20 minutes. Transfer to a serving bowl.

3   Drizzle with the dressing of your choice.

4   Serve the salad scattered with fresh mint and crumbled feta cheese.

YOU WILL NEED

1 head of cauliflower, broken into
    florets
thumb-sized piece of root ginger,
    grated
1 head of garlic
1 tbsp ground cumin
1 tbsp ground coriander
1 tsp ground turmeric
handful of sunflower seeds
handful of pumpkin seeds
pinch of salt
pinch of black pepper
2 tbsp coconut/olive oil
1–4 dried red chillies
100g/3½oz/½ cup feta cheese
handful of fresh mint leaves

Vegan Nicoise

with roasted chickpeas/garbanzo beans, potatoes and tomatoes

serves 2–4
cooking time: 25–30 minutes

Sometimes you want something a little more than a leafy salad. This dish hits all the right spots with the crispy potatoes, roasted tomatoes, crunchy chickpeas/garbanzo beans and fresh veggies combining beautifully with a delicious dressing of your choice. I make this salad with the Roasted Chickpeas/Garbanzo Beans on page 361 and the Green Goddess Dressing on page 61 but you could also try it with the Beetroot/Beet, Ginger & Lemon Sauce on page 53, the Salsa Macha on page 66 or the Ginger & Turmeric Sauce on page 46.

YOU WILL NEED

2 small potatoes, quartered

2 large tomatoes, cut into wedges

2 celery stalks, cut into strips

2 garlic cloves

couple of sprigs of fresh thyme and rosemary (i)

2 tbsp olive oil

½ cucumber, cut into chunks

½ beetroot/beet, peeled and thinly sliced

Roasted Chickpeas/Garbanzo Beans (see page 361)

125ml/4fl oz/½ cup Green Goddess Dressing (See Page 61)

METHOD

1 Preheat the grill/broiler to high.

2 Cook the potatoes in a pan of boiling salted water for 10–15 minutes until soft. You could also steam them.

3 Place the potatoes, tomatoes, celery, garlic, thyme and rosemary in a roasting pan, drizzle over the oil and grill/broil for 15 minutes until softened and charred.

4 Spoon the ingredients from the roasting tin into a salad bowl.

5 Add the cucumber, beetroot/beet and roasted chickpeas/garbanzo beans and top with the delicious dressing.

NOTE

i   This is a suggestion; other herbs such as coriander/cilantro, basil or mint will work well too.

Rainbow Salad

with heirloom carrots, beetroot/beets, radishes, tomatoes, mint, toasted almonds and strawberries

serves 4
prep time: 15 minutes

The combination of all these mind-blowingly beautiful fruits and veggies is wild. The mint adds a wonderful dimension to this salad, perfectly complementing the sweet strawberries and crunchy toasted almonds. Wherever possible, try to eat the rainbow!

If you don't have access to heirloom veggies, any standard veggies will suffice.

METHOD

1 In a large salad bowl, combine all the ingredients except the almonds and toss together.

2 Toast the almonds in a dry pan on a medium heat for 5 minutes until golden brown.

3 Combine all of the ingredients for the dressing in a jar and shake well.

4 Pour the dressing over the salad and top with toasted almonds.

YOU WILL NEED

1 candy striped beetroot/beet, thinly
   sliced
handful of strawberries, quartered
2 rainbow carrots, peeled and sliced
   into rounds
handful of cherry tomatoes, quartered
½ watermelon radish, sliced into
   rounds
2 handfuls of mixed greens
handful of mint leaves
handful of flaked/sliced almonds

FOR THE DRESSING

juice of 1 lime/lemon
1 tsp of mustard
3 tbsp olive oil
1 tsp agave/honey/coconut nectar
salt and pepper
handful of fresh oregano leaves

Weekday Quinoa Salad

with herbs, seeds and any veg you have

serves 2–4
cooking time: 20 minutes

Quinoa is an incredibly versatile ingredient. It's gluten-free, high in protein and fibre, has a low glycemic index and is one of the few plant proteins containing all nine essential amino acids. This ancient South American grain is nutritious, delicious and easy to make. Quinoa forms the base of this salad, to which you can add many different veggies and fruit, a zingy dressing, something crunchy and you'll have a wholesome meal. This salad also works beautifully with buckwheat or spelt. I find that cooking a grain such as quinoa or buckwheat and storing it in jars in the fridge for 3–5 days makes it easier to make quick, healthy, protein-filled salads.

Elevate this salad with Smoky Coconut Bacon or Dukkah on page 40 as well as the Savoury Granola on page 42, the Basil Pesto on page 57, the Green Goddess Dressing on page 61 or the Turkish Sauce on page 58.

METHOD

1 Cook the quinoa in a saucepan on a medium heat with the water. Bring to the boil, simmer until the water has evaporated, about 15 minutes, then remove from the heat. Add the tablespoon of olive oil, salt and pepper, then put the lid on to steam for 5 minutes.

2 Toss the quinoa into a large salad bowl, allow it to cool and then add your chosen ingredients. Mix well.

3 Add toppings and dressing of your choice and mix again, making sure everything is coated.

4 Serve with toasted seeds or nuts, coconut bacon and herbs for extra colour.

YOU WILL NEED

200g/7oz/1¼ cup quinoa (i)
500ml/17fl oz/2 cups water
1 tbsp olive oil
salt and pepper
handful of rocket/arugula
handful of microgreens
a few sprigs of fresh mint
6 sundried tomatoes, chopped or torn
handful of pitted olives, chopped
handful of hemp seeds
handful of black sesame seeds

OPTIONAL EXTRAS (ii)

avocado
cherry tomatoes
grilled mushrooms
cucumber
beetroot/beets
crispy onions
nectarine/pear/apple wedges
roasted veggies
spiralized courgettes/zucchini
    and carrots
any nuts/seeds, toasted
Smoky Coconut Bacon (see page 40)
Fresh basil, thyme, oregano, parsley

NOTES

i   Cooking quinoa is the same ratio as rice: 2:1 water to quinoa.

ii   This salad is wonderful just as is but also a great base and would work beautifully with any of these added ingredients.

The Crags, Plettenberg Bay, South Africa, shot on a Sony a6500 with a Mitakon Zhongyi fixed 35mm lens

Wild Rice Salad

with cucumber, beetroot/beets, greens, hummus, hibiscus flowers and romesco sauce

serves 2
prep time: 15 minutes

This salad is perfect on a summer's day. Crunchy, tangy and salty, sweet and sour in all the right places. It's made up of simple dips and sauces from the other chapters in this book and flowers that can be found in many gardens.

METHOD

1   Toast the sunflower seeds in a dry pan over a low heat for 5 minutes until golden.

2   Combine all the salad ingredients in a bowl except the hibiscus flowers.

3   Serve on two plates with a smear of hummus on each. Load the salad up, top with the hibiscus flowers, olive oil, lemon juice and lashings of the romesco sauce.

YOU WILL NEED

handful of sunflower seeds
200g/7oz/1 cup cooked wild and/or
   brown rice
1 beetroot/beet, peeled and julienned
2 handfuls of cherry tomatoes, halved
handful of pitted olives, sliced
½ cucumber, diced
2 handfuls of salad leaves/greens
2 fresh hibiscus flowers

TO SERVE
Creamy Hummus (see page 279)
1 tbsp olive oil
squeeze of lemon/lime juice
Smoky Romesco Sauce (see page 50)

273

Healing Rice Bowl

with candy striped beetroot/beets, watermelon radishes, nori and wasabi dressing

serves 1
prep time: 15 minutes

This dish requires no cooking, apart from the brown rice. Everything else is raw and combines to create the most delicious, crunchy and light meal. The saltiness of the nori, the creamy avocado, sharp radish and wasabi create a simple dish that you will want to eat over and over again. Trust me. If you are not a fan of wasabi, try one of my other sauces on page 46.

Did you know that seaweed can detox your body from heavy metals? Include more of this nutritional sea plant in your diet and learn about the ways in which you can sustainably harvest your own seaweed to add to salads, soups and stir fries.

METHOD

1 Arrange all the fresh ingredients and nori on top of the rice in a bowl, drizzle with ponzu sauce and sprinkle with sesame seeds.

2 Blend together the dressing ingredients until smooth.

3 Serve with pickled ginger and the dressing on the side.

YOU WILL NEED

200g/7oz/1 cup cooked brown rice
¼ red pepper, sliced
¼ candy striped beetroot/beet, thinly sliced
¼ watermelon radish, thinly sliced
½ avocado, cut into chunks
handful of fresh coriander/cilantro
2 spring onions/scallions, sliced
2 sheets of nori, sliced
2 tbsp ponzu sauce
sprinkle of black sesame seeds
pickled root ginger, to serve

FOR THE DRESSING

1 tsp wasabi
handful of sunflower seeds, soaked
juice of 1 lime
1 tsp coconut sugar/agave
1 tsp sesame oil
1 tsp miso
60ml/2fl oz/¼ cup water

The Amber Fort, Jaipur, Rajasthan, India, shot on a Panasonic GH4 with a fixed 50mm lens

Creamy Hummus

with olives and parsley

serves 4
cooking time: 15 minutes, plus 1½–2 hours if cooking the chickpeas/garbanzo beans

This hummus is very versatile – you could try making it with butter beans instead of chickpeas/garbanzo beans or try adding a piece of beetroot/beet, roasted peppers or carrots, a handful of sundried tomatoes, herbs or olives to change things up a bit.

Toppings like toasted nuts and seeds, spices like cumin seeds, chilli oil, lemon zest and roasted or grilled veg and fresh greens really give your hummus an extra zing.

YOU WILL NEED

2 x 400g/14oz cans of chickpeas/garbanzo beans or
    350g/12⅓oz/2 cups dried chickpeas, soaked overnight
¾ tsp bicarbonate of soda/baking soda
2 garlic cloves
4 tbsp olive oil
125ml/4fl oz/½ cup tahini
180g/6⅓oz/1 cup pitted olives
handful of fresh parsley leaves
1 tsp ground cumin
juice of ½ lemon/lime
salt and pepper

METHOD

1   Cook the dried chickpeas/garbanzo beans in a pot of boiling water on a medium heat with the bicarbonate of soda/baking soda and garlic until they are very, very soft, about 1½–2 hours. If you are using canned chickpeas, cook for 15 minutes.

2   Remove the garlic and spoon the chickpeas into a blender, leaving the water behind.

3   Blend the chickpeas, olive oil and tahini on high until smooth and creamy, adding some water as needed to loosen the hummus. You can also add an ice cube here for extra fluffiness.

4   Add the olives, parsley, cumin, lemon juice, salt and black pepper to a bowl and mix. Add 1 tablespoon of this mixture into your hummus and mix well. Serve topped with the rest of the mixture.

This is a beetroot/beet hummus topped with tahini, smoked paprika, cumin, turmeric, sesame seeds and edible flowers.

Edamame Hummus

with mint, lime and ginger topped with mushrooms and black sesame seeds

serves 4–6
prep time: 15 minutes

Edamame beans blend into the creamiest, most delicious purée that literally does a happy dance on your tongue. They are a great source of plant-based protein, fibre, antioxidants and vitamins. Get creative with different toppings as you like or add this hummus to bowls, salads, wraps and sarmies.

METHOD

1 In a food processor, pulse the edamame beans, ginger, lime juice, tahini and 1 clove of garlic.

2 Add water until you reach a creamy consistency.

3 In a frying pan on a medium heat, sauté the mushrooms, chilli and the rest of the garlic in the olive oil for 5–8 minutes until browned. Remove from the heat and add the liquid aminos or soy sauce.

4 Serve the hummus with the mushrooms spooned on top, topped with black sesame seeds and a drizzle of sesame oil.

YOU WILL NEED

350g/12⅓oz/2 cups shelled edamame beans
1 tbsp grated root ginger
juice of 1 small lime
2 tbsp tahini
4 garlic cloves, crushed
2 handfuls of mushrooms, sliced
1 red chilli, chopped
2 tbsp olive oil
2 tbsp liquid aminos/soy sauce
sprinkle of black sesame seeds
sesame oil

283

Butter Bean Hummus

with squash blossoms and moringa flowers

serves 2
prep time: 15 minutes

A hummus plate is one of my favourite light meals. Chickpeas/garbanzo beans are high in protein and when blitzed into creamy hummus and topped with all your favourite things, this humble dip becomes a meal on its own.

If you're sensitive to chickpeas, beans and lentils also work well, as do green peas and edamame beans (see Edamame Hummus on page 283). My favourite is without a doubt the creamy butter bean. This butter bean hummus is made in exactly the same way as the hummus on page 279 but uses butter beans instead of chickpeas.

Another way to serve squash blossoms is to stuff them with your favourite cheese and fry them in olive oil – the most delicious treat. Top these with toasted sunflower seeds and herb oil.

YOU WILL NEED

1 tbsp olive oil
handful of asparagus spears, woody
    ends removed, halved
handful of squash blossoms (i)
1 ripe tomato, cut into wedges
handful of pitted green olives, halved
1 tbsp lemon juice
Creamy Hummus (see page 279)
handful of moringa leaves and flowers
    (ii)
1 tbsp sunflower seeds, toasted

METHOD

1   Heat the olive oil in a frying pan on a medium heat. Add the asparagus
    and squash blossoms and sauté for 3 minutes.

2   Add the tomato slices and turn off the heat. Toss in the olives and
    lemon juice.

3   Serve on top of creamy hummus and sprinkled with moringa leaves
    (or any other greens) and toasted sunflower seeds.

NOTES

i   Any other veggies you have will also work.

ii Or any edible leaves and flowers you have.

Spice it Up

I love how each country I have visited has traditional spices that have been used in their recipes for eons. That rich and beautifully red smoked paprika from Spain, cardamom pods, cumin seeds and cloves from India and cinnamon bark and turmeric root from Sri-Lanka. Spices are so uplifting with their gorgeous aromas wafting through the air when you cook, awakening your taste buds and boosting both the flavour and medicinal benefits of the food.

Medicinal Spices

India – the multicoloured land of extremes, of unending natural beauty and unforgiving cities, a place that pulls at your core and inevitably catapults you into a state of greater self-awareness.

Travelling in India is humbling, and patience is not only a necessity but a naturally acquired art form. India is governed by unwritten rules and laws, perfect chaos where anything and nothing goes, simultaneously.

A spiritual dream that forces you to go deep within, until a beautiful light begins to shine on your soul.

Travelling through India for three months was a culinary delight of dreams.

Indian food seduced me and made me think about plant-based food in a whole new way; from Baingan masala (aubergine/eggplant) to Bombay aloo (spicy turmeric potatoes), rich and creamy dhal makhani (black urad lentils cooked slowly for a smoky, creamy flavour) and perfectly spiced coconut rotis, to light and crispy masala dosas (rice pancake with potatoes and green coconut chilli chutney).

Indian food is a labour of love, passion and intention. The lentils are cooked with powerful ayurvedic spices to make them easier to digest; these healing blends work to balance your body in magical ways.

Cooking is a meditation, something to be savoured and adored and India made me feel this even more.

Ayurvedic cooking in India enriched my understanding of the idea of food as medicine. There are incredible spices for pretty much every ailment, and spices and ingredients that are specifically combined with certain foods to make the food more digestible. I have added notes to most of the recipes in this section regarding the healing properties of various ayurvedic ingredients.

Leh, Ladakh, India, shot on a Panasonic GH4 with a fixed 50mm lens

NOTES

i   It's best to soak nuts overnight, but a quick soak in boiling water for
    15–30 minutes will suffice.

ii Chestnut/cremini, shiitake, portobellini, oyster or wild mushrooms.

iii Hemp, pumpkin, sunflower, sesame or a mixture pulsed in
    a food processor until ground.

Wild Mushroom Rice Ball

with creamy spinach sauce

serves 2-4
cooking time: 25 minutes

This is almost like arancini (Italian fried risotto balls) or Spanish bombas (mashed potato stuffed with cheese and deep-fried).

My version is brown rice with lots of nutritious seeds, like hemp and sesame, wild mushrooms, spring onions/scallions and fresh herbs. The mixture binds using chia gel and coconut flour. The rice ball is served in a bowl of spinach sauce, based on the Indian palak, with lots of ginger and spices. This sauce also works deliciously with chickpeas/garbanzo beans, mushrooms, potatoes, paneer, tofu or aubergine/eggplant.

If using potatoes, you would simply boil them and then spice them up with 1–4 teaspoons each of turmeric, chilli, cumin and coriander before tossing in the sauce.

METHOD

1 For the spinach sauce, steam or simmer the spinach in water for 1 minute until wilted but still bright green. Rinse in cold water and place in a blender. Toast the spices in a dry pan on a medium heat for 1–2 minutes until fragrant, then add to the blender with the other ingredients. Blend until smooth.

2 To make the spinach balls, in a frying pan on a medium heat, sauté the onion, garlic, ginger and spices in coconut oil for 3–4 minutes until golden and fragrant. Add the mushrooms and fry for 5 minutes until browned.

3 Mix the chia seeds with the water in a cup and set aside for about 10 minutes until a gel forms.

4 Combine the brown rice and seeds with the mushroom mixture in a bowl, add the coconut flour, chia gel and any extra veg.

5 Use your hands to mould the mixture into 4 balls and roll them in more coconut flour and seeds. Fry in a little olive oil on a medium heat until golden brown on each side, about 3–5 minutes.

6 Warm the spinach sauce in a saucepan, but keep an eye on it so it doesn't lose its green colour. Serve the fried balls in bowls of the creamy spinach sauce.

YOU WILL NEED

FOR THE SPINACH SAUCE
120g/4¼oz/4 cups spinach
1 tsp ground coriander
1 tsp ground cumin
1 tsp chilli powder
1 tbsp garam masala spice mix
　(see page 308)
2 garlic cloves
thumb-sized piece of root ginger, peeled and grated
handful of sunflower seeds/cashew nuts, soaked (i)
juice of 1 lemon

FOR THE SPINACH BALLS
1 red onion, diced
2 garlic cloves
thumb-sized piece of root ginger
1 tsp cumin seeds
1 tsp ground turmeric
2 tbsp coconut oil
2 handfuls of mushrooms, chopped (ii)
2 tsp chia seeds
75ml/2½fl oz/⅓ cup water
200g/7oz/1 cup cooked brown/wild rice
handful of seeds, plus more for rolling (iii)
50g/1¾oz/½ cup coconut flour, plus more for rolling
olive oil

OPTIONAL EXTRAS
handful of sliced red cabbage
handful of spinach leaves

Kitchari

perfectly spiced and healing Ayurvedic dhal with two-ingredient naan

serves 6
cooking time: 1 hour 15 minutes

Ayurveda is the ancient healing science that forms part of the same tradition as yoga.

Kitchari is an uplifting, detoxing dhal that is a daily staple in Ayurvedic cooking. A perfect combination of carbohydrates, protein and healing spices results in a dhal that is truly transformational and balanced. This medicinal food is wonderful for colds and flu, detoxing, inflammation, infection, digestive disturbances and balancing of hormones.

METHOD

1   Rinse and drain the mung beans until the water runs clear, about 5 times.

2   Heat the ghee or oil in a large saucepan on a medium heat, then add the black mustard, cumin seeds, fennel and fenugreek seeds. Toast until the mustard seeds pop, about 1 minute.

3   Add turmeric, black pepper, ground cumin, coriander and cinnamon and mix together. Stir in the rice and rinsed beans.

4   Add the water, chopped vegetables, cloves, bay leaves and cardamom pods. Bring to the boil for 5 minutes, then reduce to a simmer. Cook for at least 1 hour, until the beans and rice are soft and the kitchari has a porridge-like consistency.

5   Serve warm with fresh coriander/cilantro, if using.

YOU WILL NEED

750 g/1lb 10oz/4 cups yellow mung dhal beans (i)

3 tbsp ghee/organic sesame oil

4 tsp black mustard seeds

4 tsp cumin seeds

2 tsp fennel seeds

2 tsp fenugreek seeds

4 tsp ground turmeric

4 tsp ground black pepper

2 tsp ground cumin

2 tsp ground coriander

2 tsp ground cinnamon

350g/12⅓oz/2 cups white basmati rice

2 litres/70fl oz/8½ cups water

2–5 handfuls of organic seasonal vegetables, chopped (ii)

2 cloves

4 bay leaves

6 green cardamom pods

2 handfuls of fresh coriander/cilantro leaves, chopped (optional)

NOTES

i   Alternatively, use the red split
    lentil variety.

ii   Such as spinach, carrots, beetroot/beets,
    sweet potato, squash, celery, kale, and pak
    choi/bok choy (avoid all nightshades).

Naan Bread

makes 4-6 naans
cooking time: 45 minutes–1 hour

These two-ingredient naan breads are so easy to make and impossible to mess up. The yoghurt adds a slight tanginess that is characteristic of naan bread and the acidity in the yoghurt helps to break down the gluten resulting in a softer, more pliable dough. These naans are even more delicious when brushed with coconut oil or garlic butter before serving.

YOU WILL NEED

240g/9oz/2 cups self-raising flour
250g/9oz/1 cup plain or coconut yoghurt

METHOD

1 Sift the flour into a bowl and mix in the yoghurt with a wooden spoon until well combined.

2 Sprinkle your work surface with flour and then knead for 3–5 minutes until smooth. Knead into a ball, adding extra flour if the dough is too sticky. Allow to rest in the fridge for 15–30 minutes (you can skip this part if you're pressed for time).

3 Cut or break the dough into palm-sized pieces and roll out using a rolling pin, sprinkling flour over the bread and work surface to prevent it from sticking.

4 Heat a cast iron pan on a medium to high heat. When hot, dry cook the the naan breads on one side, until golden, about 1–2 mnutes, then flip and cook for a further 1–2 minutes on the other side.

Tadka/Tempering

This final stage in an Indian dhal or curry takes the flavour to a whole new level. Simply sauté ginger, garlic, chilli and spices of your choice in coconut oil, ghee or butter until fragrant. I usually use cumin seeds, mustard seeds, masala spice and sometimes something crunchy like flaked almonds. Pour this sizzling hot sauce over your curry before serving.

Dhal Tadka

yellow lentils with cumin-roasted carrots, barley, toasted seeds and greens

serves 4
cooking time: 35 minutes

Lentils in any form have been a go-to for me for years. They are cost-effective, wholesome and filling. Lentils form a perfect protein when combined with brown rice or other grains, such as barley. Your options are endless.

Cook a pan of lentils on a Sunday to last you the week and be creative with variations. This curry has the addition of simple roasted carrots in it, but roasted cauliflower would work well too. I like to serve this with cooked barley (or choose your favourite grain), toasted pumpkin seeds, a handful of fresh coriander/cilantro, edible flowers, spring onions/scallions and the Coconut Sambal or Spicy Indian Almonds on page 41.

METHOD

1 Preheat the oven to 180°C/350°F/Gas 4.

2 In a roasting pan, coat the carrots in half the cumin seeds, salt and pepper and roast in 2 tablespoons of the coconut oil until golden brown, about 20 minutes.

3 Toast the mustard seeds, ground coriander and turmeric in a dry pan on a medium heat for 1–2 minutes until fragrant.

4 Add the coconut oil, the onion, half the ginger and half the garlic to the pan and sauté until golden brown, around 5 minutes.

5 Add the tomatoes and simmer for 5 minutes. Add the lentils and water. Turn the heat up to high and bring to the boil. Cook for 20 minutes until the lentils have softened.

6 Turn the heat down, add the milk or cream, peas, salt and pepper and roasted carrots. Allow the peas to soften with the lid on for 1–2 minutes.

7 For the ultimate fragrant taste explosion, add the finishing temper to the curry: fry up the other half of the cumin seeds, ginger and garlic and the halved red chilli in coconut oil on a medium heat for 1–2 minutes until golden and fragrant. You can also add a handful of chopped nuts or seeds to the oil. Pour over the curry before serving.

YOU WILL NEED

4 large carrots, peeled

1 tbsp cumin seeds

salt and pepper

1 tsp yellow mustard seeds

1 tbsp ground coriander

1 tbsp ground turmeric

4 tbsp coconut oil

1 onion, chopped

thumb-sized piece of root ginger, diced

4 garlic cloves, diced

400g/14oz can of chopped tomatoes

500g/1lb 2oz/2½ cups lentils (red or yellow), rinsed

750ml/26fl oz/3¼ cups water

400ml/14fl oz can of coconut cream/ milk

160g/5⅔oz/1¼ cup frozen garden peas

1 red chilli, halved lengthways

JOURNAL ENTRY//

In an alleyway off Khao San Road in Bangkok, I sat staring into the eyes
of an Indian psychic. "You will visit my country many times," he said.
India, you are such a wild inspiration and healing journey in my life,
I long to return to your chaos and peace, magic and misery, a cracking
open of the heart and peeling back of layers like never before. Reminiscing
on moments shared; from your mystical mountains, sleepy apple orchard
villages in the Himalayas, icy blue lakes in the stark landscape of the north
and delicious influences of Tibetan cuisine. Nostalgia, filtering into the
alluring scents and tastes, letting our senses experience that of ancient
civilisations with incredible enlightenment in the ruins of Hampi, stirring
images of golden days where time was cherished and spent doing that
which enriched and enlightened rather than enslaved. In these moments,
feeding into how addicted I am to your very essence, I felt at home in
your embrace and know that I will return to your magic.

Hampi, India, shot on a Panasonic GH4 with a fixed 50mm lens

Green Mango Dhal

with quick pickled onions and blueberry chilli jam

serves 4
cooking time: 20 minutes

This dhal is made with green mango, which cooks at the same time as the lentils and gives a tangy, slightly sour element to the dish. I absolutely love it for its simplicity and celebration of just a few magical ingredients.

Did you know that lentils on their own are not a complete protein? When combined with a grain like barley or rice they contain all the necessary amino acids to form a complete protein.

The blueberry chilli jam goes so well with this dhal but any chutney, chilli jam, atchar or relish will be equally delicious.

METHOD

1   In a saucepan, cover the lentils with water and soak for 20 minutes. Rinse until the water runs clear, drain and cover the lentils with more water (1–1.5litres/ 35-50fl oz/4–6 cups). Add the mango, half the ginger, half the turmeric and the pepper. Simmer on a medium to high heat until the lentils and mango are soft, about 15–20 minutes. Add water if necessary, depending on how thick you like your dhal. Remove from the heat. Use the back of a spoon or vegetable masher to mix the mangoes and lentils together.

2   In a frying pan on a medium heat, fry the remaining turmeric, red chillies, mustard and cumin seeds in the oil for 1 minute until fragrant. Add the garlic, remaining ginger and a pinch of salt and fry for 1–2 minutes until golden brown. Pour over the top of your dhal before serving.

3   Place the chilli jam ingredients in a pot on a low heat and simmer for 10 minutes until reduced and sticky.

4   For the quick pickled onions, soak the onion slices in the vinegar, water and coconut sugar until they turn pink, about 10 minutes.

5   Serve the dhal topped with the blueberry chilli jam and the pickled onions.

YOU WILL NEED

400g/14oz/2 cups yellow/red lentils
1 green mango, peeled and chopped
    into small cubes
thumb-sized piece of root ginger,
    chopped
1 tbsp ground turmeric
salt and black pepper
1–2 dried red chillies
1 tbsp mustard seeds
2 tbsp cumin seeds
2 tbsp coconut oil/ghee/olive oil
6 garlic cloves, chopped

FOR THE BLUEBERRY CHILLI JAM

2 handfuls of blueberries
1 tsp coconut sugar
1 tsp red chilli flakes
1 tsp grated garlic
1 tsp grated root ginger
75ml/2½fl oz/⅓ cup water
salt and pepper

FOR THE QUICK PICKLED ONIONS

1 onion, sliced
2 tbsp vinegar
2 tbsp water
1 tsp coconut sugar

Mushroom Biryani

with mint, peanuts and quick mango chutney

serves 4
cooking time: 25 minutes

This biryani warms my heart every time. The mushrooms and mint are a perfect combination with the sweet, spicy zing of the mango chutney. The smell of Indian spices dreamily floating through the air reminds me of times in the Himalayas, on the banks of the Ganges, or in the lush jungles of Rishikesh.

Traditionally, biryani is made by layering rice, vegetables, herbs and spices in a pot and then cooked on a low heat with a lid on. In this recipe I have combined the flavours of Biryani with the technique of a fried rice to save on time and cooking steps.

METHOD

1 Add the rice, cinnamon, cloves, cardamom, bay leaves and water to a saucepan and cook according to rice's package instructions.

2 Grind all the spices (excluding cinnamon, cloves and cardamom) in a pestle and mortar, coffee grinder or blender until fine.

3 Toast this spice mixture in a dry pan on a medium heat until fragrant, about 2 minutes.

4 Add the coconut oil, ginger and onion and sauté until golden brown, 5–10 minutes.

5 Add the mushrooms and garlic and sauté until they are brown and tender, about 5 minutes.

6 Add the rice and stir through until warm. Top with toasted peanuts and fresh mint, lemon or lime juice and zest and a spoonful of mango chutney.

7 To make the mango chutney - In a saucepan on a low heat, stir together all the ingredients and cook down for 15 minutes until reduced and sticky.

YOU WILL NEED

400g/14oz/2 cups basmati rice
1 cinnamon stick
8 cloves
6–8 cardamom pods
2–4 bay leaves
1 tsp ground turmeric
1 tsp cumin seeds
1 tsp coriander seeds
1 tsp dried red chilli
1 tsp fennel seeds
1 tsp black pepper
2 tbsp coconut oil
thumb-sized piece of root ginger, chopped
1 onion, diced
200g/7oz/2 cups mushrooms, sliced
6 garlic cloves, chopped
handful of raw unsalted peanuts, toasted
handful of fresh mint leaves
zest and juice of 1 lemon/lime

FOR THE MANGO CHUTNEY

1 mango, diced
1 red onion, diced
1 tsp ground turmeric
1 tsp black mustard seeds
1 tbsp coconut sugar
1 tbsp grated root ginger
juice of 1 lemon/lime
100ml/3½fl oz/scant ½ cup water

Leh, Ladakh India, shot on a Panasonic GH4 with a fixed 50mm lens

Coconut Curry

with fresh coconut chunks, cauliflower and potato

serves 4
cooking time: 25 minutes

A simple masala mixed with fresh coconut, potato and cauliflower, served with fresh coriander/cilantro and some wild rice. A delicious and quick curry that is affordable too.

METHOD

1   Parboil the potatoes in a pan of boiling salted water for about 10 minutes until soft but still firm in the centres.

2   For the garam masala spice mix, toast all the spices in a dry pan for about 2 minutes until fragrant. Remove from the heat and pulse in a food processor, coffee grinder or use a pestle and mortar to blend into a powder.

3   For the curry, in a pan on a medium heat, fry the onion, ginger and garlic in 4 tablespoons of the masala spice mixture and the coconut oil for about 5 minutes until the spices smell fragrant and the onions are browned. Add the cauliflower and coconut and stir, coating in the spice mixture. Cook for another 5 minutes until golden.

4   Add the tomatoes, coconut sugar, water and the potatoes and allow to simmer for 10 minutes, until the sauce thickens.

5   Serve with wild rice and scattered with fresh coriander/cilantro.

YOU WILL NEED

2 large potatoes, peeled

1 onion, diced

thumb-sized piece of root ginger, diced

2 garlic cloves, diced

2–4 tbsp coconut oil

100g/3½oz/1 cup cauliflower, chopped

80g/2¾oz/1 cup fresh brown coconut, cut into chunky slices

4 tomatoes, diced

1 tsp coconut sugar

250ml/9fl oz/1 cup water

400g/14oz/2 cups cooked wild rice

handful of fresh coriander/cilantro

FOR THE GARAM MASALA SPICE MIX

½ tbsp fennel seeds

½ tbsp ground turmeric

½ tbsp red chilli flakes

½ tbsp coriander seeds

½ tbsp cumin seeds

½ tbsp whole black peppercorns

8 cardamom pods

½ tsp mustard seeds

Leh, Ladakh, India, shot on a Panasonic GH4 with a fixed 50mm lens

Mushroom Masala

serves 2
cooking time: 20 minutes

The warming spices in this dish are particularly healing in nature. Mushrooms are a source of protein and, when served with a whole grain such as brown rice, provide a balanced meal that is wholesome and nourishing.

This is delicious with sunflower seed cream drizzled on top. Combine 1 handful of toasted sunflower seeds with a small garlic clove, the juice of half a lemon, salt, pepper and a glug of olive oil and water as needed. Alternatively use coconut cream. I also like to top this with raw greens smothered in lemon juice.

YOU WILL NEED

2 tbsp garam masala spice mix (see page 308)

2 tbsp coconut oil

1 onion, diced

thumb-sized piece of root ginger, diced

4–6 garlic cloves, diced

2–4 handfuls of your favourite mushrooms, left whole or torn into bite sized pieces

4 ripe tomatoes, blended

250–500ml/9–17fl oz/1–2 cups water

juice of 1 lime/lemon

1 tsp coconut sugar

400g/14oz/2 cups cooked basmati rice

handful of fresh coriander/cilantro

METHOD

1 Fry the spice mix in the coconut oil until fragrant, about 1-2 minutes.

2 Add the onion, ginger and garlic and sauté on a medium heat for 4–5 minutes until golden.

3 Toss in the mushrooms and brown for 5–8 minutes. Add the tomatoes, 250ml/9fl oz/1 cup of the water, lime juice and sugar and simmer for 5 minutes. Add the remaining water and simmer for a further 10 minutes until the sauce has thickened and reduced.

4 Serve with basmati rice and coriander/cilantro.

Thai Massaman Curry

with peanut, potato, pineapple and coconut

serves 4
cooking time: 20 minutes

Thai food is truly something special, with the perfect balance of sweet, sour and salty – it all comes together to do happy dances on your tongue. My memories of Thailand are all centered around food, from roadside Creamy Tom Yum (see page 143), to som tum (green papaya) salad and coconut shakes.

This massaman curry takes me back to scooter trips through palm tree forests, warm oceans, hot, humid days and the friendly faces of local Thai people. I took the liberty of adding pineapple to this curry, which turned out to be a delicious addition, but it is not traditionally included in this dish.

YOU WILL NEED

4 potatoes, peeled and quartered
2–4 tbsp Thai massaman paste
2 tbsp coconut oil
I onion, chopped
4 handfuls raw unsalted peanuts
2–4 lime leaves
½ pineapple, cut into chunks
400ml/14fl oz can of coconut milk
100ml/3½fl oz/scant ½ cup water
2 handfuls of desiccated/dried
   shredded coconut
handful of fresh coriander/cilantro
lime wedges, to serve

METHOD

1   Parboil the potatoes in a pan of boiling salted water for about 10 minutes until soft but still firm in the centres.

2   In a wok on a medium heat, fry the curry paste in the coconut oil for 2–3 minutes until fragrant. Add the onion, half of the peanuts and the lime leaves and sauté for 5 minutes until golden.

3   Toss the potatoes and pineapple in, adding the coconut milk and water. Simmer for 10 minutes.

4   Crush the remainder of the peanuts or pulse in a food processor until fine. Toast the peanuts and coconut in a dry pan on a medium heat for 5 minutes until golden.

5   Serve the curry with the toasted peanuts and coconut, fresh coriander/cilantro and a squeeze of lime juice with a lime wedge on the side.

Chile Relleno

stuffed with sweet potato mash, served on ratatouille

serves 2
cooking time: 40 minutes

Chile relleno is traditionally battered and fried peppers stuffed with cheese, shrimp or any other meat and served with a delicious spicy tomato sauce and rice. This recipe is a healthier version, but if you would like to keep it traditional, whisk together 60g/2¼oz/½ cup flour, 100ml/3½fl oz/scant ½ cup water, lemon zest and a pinch of salt. Coat your stuffed pepper in the batter and fry until golden. If you are doing it this way, make sure to grill/broil your pepper first until soft, before stuffing and frying.

You could try stuffing the pepper with other combinations such as cheese and tofu, roasted chickpeas/garbanzo beans and cheese or cashew cream and mushrooms. Instead of the ratatouille, a simple salsa roja can be made by cooking 300g/10½oz/2 cups cherry tomatoes, 1 finely chopped onion, 2 crushed garlic cloves, 1 tsp cumin seeds, 1 tsp dried chilli, 3 tbsp olive oil and 1 tbsp butter in a pan for 10 minutes. Add 120ml/4fl oz/½ cup water and 1 tbsp tomato purée/paste and blitz in a blender until smooth.

METHOD

1   Preheat the grill/broiler to high.

2   Cook the sweet potatoes in a pan of boiling salted water for 15–20 minutes until soft. Drain the water and mash the sweet potato, adding 1 tablespoon of olive oil, salt and pepper.

3   Stuff the peppers with a spoonful or two of the sweet potato, then drizzle with 1 tablespoon of the olive oil and nutritional yeast. Place the stuffed peppers in an ovenproof dish and grill/broil for 20 minutes.

4   Meanwhile, make the ratatouille. In a frying pan on a medium heat, sauté the onion, garlic and cumin seeds in 2 tablespoons of the olive oil for about 5 minutes until golden. Add the tomatoes, courgette/zucchini and water and simmer for 20 minutes until thickened.

5   Drizzle the cucumber with the remaining 1 tablespoon of olive oil and lemon juice and season with salt and pepper.

6   Serve the stuffed peppers on the ratatouille with the cucumber salad as a side and a generous wedge of avocado.

YOU WILL NEED

2 large sweet potatoes, peeled and
    quartered
4 tbsp olive oil
salt and pepper, to taste
2 large green peppers, deseeded (i)
1 tbsp nutritional yeast
1 onion, diced
2 garlic cloves, diced
1 tsp cumin seeds
2 handfuls of cherry tomatoes,
    chopped
1 courgette/zucchini, diced
125ml/4fl oz/½ cup water
¼ cucumber, grated
Juice of 1 lemon/lime
½ avocado, cut into wedges, to serve

NOTE

i   Mexican red poblano peppers are
    traditionally used, but any green,
    yellow or red peppers will do.

The ancients believed that food is information for our cells and assimilated into our beings to raise our awareness and consciousness.

Srinagar, Kashmir, Northern India, shot on a Panasonic GH4 with a fixed 50mm lens

Bombay Potatoes

serves 4
cooking time: 25 minutes

These potatoes are golden, delicious and moreish. Soft and fluffy, spicy and comforting – definitely one of my favourite ways to eat potatoes. The curry leaves and spices fried in coconut oil are the key to this magically simple dish.

YOU WILL NEED

4 potatoes, quartered
handful of curry leaves
2 tsp ground turmeric
2 tsp cumin seeds
1 tsp red chilli powder
1 tsp black pepper
1 tsp salt
2 tbsp coconut oil

METHOD

1 Cook the potatoes in a pan of boiling salted water for 15–20 minutes until soft, then drain.

2 In a pan on a medium heat, fry the rest of the ingredients in the oil until fragrant and golden, around 2 minutes.

3 Add the spices to the potatoes, then place the lid on the pan and shake until coated.

Brown Lentils

with healing spices

serves 4
cooking time: 45 minutes

Brown lentils are the first lentils I ever ate. This is a simple and affordable Indian-style brown lentil dhal. The most important thing to remember when using brown lentils is to soak them overnight as this breaks down the phytic acid. Unlike red lentils – which are generally the split pea variety and cook very quickly – brown lentils take more time to cook and need longer soaking.

I like to serve this with fresh greens, cucumber and red onion slices and rice.

METHOD

1　Toast the spices in a dry pan on a medium heat for 1–2 minutes until fragrant. Add the coconut oil, ginger, garlic and onion and fry for 5 minutes until golden.

2　Add the chopped tomatoes and coconut sugar and simmer for 5 minutes.

3　Add the lentils and water, bring to the boil and cook for 30 minutes until the lentils are soft.

4　Add the coconut milk and turn the heat down a further 5–10 minutes until the sauce thickens.

5　For the tempering, fry up the ingredients in coconut oil for 1–2 minutes until golden and pour over the curry before serving.

YOU WILL NEED

2 tbsp garam masala spice mix (see page 308)
1 tsp ground turmeric
1 tsp red chilli powder
2 tbsp coconut oil
2 thumb-sized pieces of root ginger, diced
4–6 garlic cloves, diced
1 onion, diced
4 ripe tomatoes, chopped
1 tsp coconut sugar
500g/1lb 2oz/2½ cups dried brown lentils, soaked overnight
750ml/26fl oz/3¼ cups water
250ml/9fl oz/1 cup coconut milk

TEMPERING

2 tbsp coconut oil
1–2 red chillies, split lengthways
1 tbsp cumin seeds
2 garlic cloves, sliced

322

Vashisht, Himachal Pradesh, India,
shot on a Panasonic GH4 with a fixed 50mm lens

On the Side

I love a side dish and this chapter is a testament to how much I love potatoes – try the Half Baked Potatoes on page 342, the Hasselbacks on page 357 or the Perfect Roasties on page 332 if you love potatoes as much as I do. There's also a lovely Broccoli Bake on page 328, Asian-inspired Grilled/Broiled Cabbage Wedges on page 341 and a simple Sri Lankan Green Beans and Tomato on page 358 that is scrumptious and sure to become a favourite. These sides would work well alongside any of the salads, plant proteins or one pot wonders in the book.

Broccoli Bake

with a creamy sunflower seed sauce and toasted almonds

serves 4
cooking time: 20 minutes

I love this dish because it reminds me of a classic cauliflower or broccoli cheese. Instead of milk and flour, you use sunflower seeds blended with water and a couple of other delicious things, like nutritional yeast and garlic. I have a feeling you're going to love it.

This cheese sauce is delicious with cashews too, but sunflower seeds are lower in fat than cashews and so much more affordable, so they really are a wonderful alternative. Dry toast the sunflower seeds for a nuttier flavour.

METHOD

1   Preheat the grill/broiler to high.

2   Steam the broccoli and cauliflower in a steamer for 5–10 minutes until tender. Arrange in an ovenproof dish.

3   In a blender, combine the sauce ingredients until creamy, adding more sunflower seeds or water to reach your desired creamy consistency.

4   Pour the cheese sauce over the broccoli and cauliflower and top with almond slices, nutritional yeast, salt and pepper.

5   Grill/broil for about 10 minutes until golden.

NOTE

i   Quick soak the cashews in boiled water for 15–30 minutes for easier blending.

ii   This adds an extra cheesy element to the sauce, but is completely optional.

YOU WILL NEED

½ head of broccoli
½ head of cauliflower
handful of flaked/sliced almonds
1 tbsp nutritional yeast
salt and pepper

FOR THE SUNFLOWER SEED CHEESE SAUCE

2 big handfuls of sunflower seeds or cashew nuts, soaked (i)
1 tsp nutritional yeast (ii) (optional)
1 garlic clove
juice of ½ lemon
250ml/9fl oz/1 cup water
palm-sized piece of yellow pepper
1 tsp mustard/mustard seeds
salt and pepper

Polenta/Cornmeal Chips

dunked in a lemony guacamole

serves 4
cooking time: 35 minutes

I had been wanting to try these baked polenta/cornmeal chips for ages, and when I finally did, I wished I had been eating them forever. I add thyme and garlic to these and dip them in a really lemony guacamole that pairs wonderfully with the rich creamy polenta.

METHOD

1 Grease and line a 20cm/8in square baking pan.

2 Bring the stock to the boil in a saucepan over a medium heat and slowly whisk in the polenta/cornmeal, stirring constantly. Add a pinch of salt and, once the polenta has thickened after 3-4 minutes of stirring, stir in the nutritional yeast and oregano.

3 Pour into the greased and lined baking pan and pop in the fridge to chill and firm up, about 1 hour.

4 Preheat the oven to 220°C/425°F/Gas 7.

5 Cut the chilled polenta into chips/fries/wedges and brush with 2 tablespoons of olive oil. Dust with the extra polenta. Arrange on a greased baking sheet in a single layer and bake for 30 minutes, or until crisp and golden, flipping half way through.

6 Mash together the guacamole ingredients with a fork until smooth and creamy and serve alongside the polenta chips for dipping.

YOU WILL NEED

400ml/14fl oz/1⅔ cups vegetable stock
150g/5½oz/1 cup quick-cook polenta/cornmeal, plus 2 tbsp for dusting
salt and pepper
2 tbsp nutritional yeast
2 tsp dried oregano
olive oil

FOR THE GUACAMOLE

2 avocados
juice of ½ lemon/lime
good glug of olive oil
pinch of paprika
salt and pepper

Perfect Roasties

in avocado oil with fresh tomato sauce

serving quantity is up to you!
cooking time: 60 minutes

I have a love affair with potatoes. In all their glorious forms, they comfort me and calm my soul. These are crispy on the outside and soft and fluffy on the inside, perfectly cooled by the raw tomato sauce.

Good-quality homegrown or organic potatoes make all the difference here. Heirloom varieties of potatoes are beautiful, and I hope you get to try them or grow them soon. From pink to purple, yellow and cream, if you've never seen them in the flesh before, you will be amazed.

This recipe is here for you to adapt to your serving requirements – make as many or as little as you want. I've added how much oil you'd need for 4–5 potatoes, but it's really up to you how much you make, so alter these quantities to your preferences!

METHOD

1 Preheat the oven to 180°C/350°F/Gas 4.

2 As you peel the potatoes, place them in a bowl of cold water until the oven has preheated. Soaking potatoes in cold water helps remove some of the excess surface starch and lead to a crisper texture.

3 Dry them off well with a dish towel. Heat enough of the avocado oil in a cast iron pan on a medium heat to shallow fry the potatoes. Add the potatoes and cook until golden brown, about 3 minutes on each side.

4 Transfer to a roasting pan and roast for 45 minutes. Once cooked, drain on paper towel and season generously with salt.

5 Blend the sauce ingredients until smooth and serve with your perfect roasties.

YOU WILL NEED

4–5 potatoes, peeled and cut into
    quarters
60–120ml/2–4 fl oz/¼ –½ cup
    avocado oil
salt

FOR THE TOMATO CHILLI SAUCE

2 ripe tomatoes/1–2 handfuls of cherry
    tomatoes
1 tbsp olive oil
1 garlic clove
½ tsp chopped chilli
½ tsp coconut sugar/agave

Bahía Concepción, Baja California Sur, shot on a Sony a6500 with a Mitakon Zhongyi fixed 35mm lens

Spicy Baked Aubergine/ Eggplant

with green herb sauce and microgreens

serves 2
cooking time: 45 minutes

These baked aubergines/eggplants are crispy and spicy with a soft centre. I like to serve them with a cooling green herb dressing like the Green Goddess Dressing on page 61, but you could also try the Creamy Mushroom Sauce on page 75 or the Smoky Romesco Sauce on page 50.

Try these with my Herby Oat and Sweet Potato Balls on page 221, Beetroot/Beet Balls on page 186, curries or Seitan Cutlets on page 198. Sometimes veggies done simply with a cracking sauce is all you need in life.

METHOD

1 Preheat the oven to 200°C/400°F/Gas 6.

2 Score the aubergine/eggplant horizontally and diagonally. Arrange the aubergine slices in an ovenproof dish and spread the salsa macha over the top. Bake for 45 minutes until golden brown and soft on the inside. Turn halfway through.

3 Serve the baked aubergine with the dressing spooned over the top and microgreens on the side.

NOTE

i You can do the same with sweet potato or potato.

YOU WILL NEED

1 large aubergine/eggplant, sliced
    lengthways (i)
2 tbsp Salsa Macha (see page 66)
125ml/4fl oz/½ cup Green Goddess
    Dressing (see page 61)
2 handfuls of microgreens

Roast Veggies

with green pesto

serves 4
cooking time: 35 minutes

You can whack these roast vegetables in the oven and forget about them. Once you're ready to eat, quickly pulse the pesto ingredients and you have a hassle-free side that is magically delicious every time.

Turn this scrumptious side into a veggie roast dinner by adding one or two of the sauces from the Dressed Up section. I recommend the Turkish Sauce (see page 58) or some drizzles of Carrot Top Chimichurri (see page 79) with the Green Olive Tapenade (see page 54).

Cooking in cast iron pans is a really good idea, as they contain no harmful toxic substances like non-stick pans do.

METHOD

1 Preheat the oven to 180°C/350°F/Gas 4.

2 Place all the vegetables in an ovenproof dish or large roasting pan, drizzle with olive oil and sprinkle with the spices and salt and pepper.

3 Roast for 35–45 minutes until golden and softened.

4 Pulse the pesto ingredients in a food processor until chunky but combined.

5 Serve the veggies with the pesto.

NOTE

i   Rocket/arugula, basil, spinach or kale would all work well.

YOU WILL NEED

1 bunch of rainbow carrots, halved
    lengthways
1 large radish, sliced
1 bunch of leeks
4 tbsp olive oil
1 tsp cumin seeds
1 tsp coriander seeds, crushed
pinch of red chilli flakes
salt and pepper

FOR THE PESTO

handful of greens (i)
2 large garlic cloves, peeled
2 handfuls of pumpkin seeds/
    sunflower seeds/nuts
pinch of salt and pepper
juice of 1 lemon
125ml/4fl oz/½ cup olive oil

Grilled/Broiled Cabbage Wedges

serves 4
cooking time: 30 minutes

Purple cabbage is rich in vitamin K and C, fights inflammation and promotes heart and gut health. These cabbage wedges are a beautiful side with wonderful flavour. They work so well on the braai or barbeque, cooked in a griddle/grill pan or grilled/broiled in the oven. Serve with the Green Goddess Dressing on page 61, the Peanut Dipping Sauce on page 72, the Beetroot/ Beet & Almond Dip on page 71 or the BBQ Sauce on page 62 with a crunchy topping like the Peanut, Lime & Chilli, Asian Crunch or Coconut Sambal on page 41.

YOU WILL NEED

1 purple cabbage, cut into wedges
2 tbsp sesame oil (i)
4 tbsp liquid aminos/soy sauce
2 red chillies, sliced
handful of sesame seeds

METHOD

1   If grilling/broiling in the oven, preheat the grill/broiler to high.

2   Drizzle the cabbage wedges with sesame oil and soy sauce and scatter over the red chilli slices.

3   Cook on the braai or barbeque for about 20–30 minutes until browned on each side. Alternatively use a griddle/grill pan or pop them under the grill for 10-15 minutes, turning occasionally, until both sides are golden and the centres are cooked through.

4   Finish with a generous sprinkling of sesame seeds.

NOTE

i   Coconut oil also works.

Half Baked Potatoes

with walnuts, garlic and rosemary and raw tomato salsa

serves 4

cooking time: 30 minutes

I love these potatoes because they're a little different from the ordinary yet easy to make.

Rosemary and potatoes are a match made in heaven. Go wild and enjoy these babies as a side or make them the star of the show by loading them up with some greens and veg and the Creamy Mushroom Sauce on page 75 or the Green Olive Tapenade on page 54.

METHOD

1   Preheat the oven to 180°C/350°F/Gas 4.

2   Parboil the potatoes in a pan of boiling salted water for about 10 minutes until soft but still firm in the centres.

2   Meanwhile, in a food processor, pulse all the ingredients for the potato topping until chunky but combined.

3   Drain the potatoes and transfer to an ovenproof dish or large roasting pan and smother with the potato topping. Pop them straight into the oven for about 15–20 minutes or until the topping is golden brown.

4   Serve the baked potatoes with the raw tomato sauce on the side.

YOU WILL NEED

4 potatoes, sliced in half lengthways
Raw Tomato Sauce (see page 216)

FOR THE POTATO TOPPING

2 sprigs of rosemary, leaves picked
4 garlic cloves
2 tbsp olive oil
2 tbsp nutritional yeast
2 handfuls of walnuts
juice of 1 lemon/lime
salt and pepper

Todos Santos, Baja California Sur, shot on a sony a6500 with a Mitakon Zhongyi fixed 35mm lens

Beetroot/Beet Chips

roasted with rosemary and chilli and served with guacamole

serves 2
cooking time: 45 minutes

I love these beetroot/beet chips. The same method would work really well with other root veggies such as carrots, sweet potatoes, potatoes, yuca or yams.

METHOD

1   Preheat the oven to 180°C/350°F/Gas 4.

2   Peel the beetroots/beets and thinly slice into rounds using a mandolin (if you don't have one, by hand works too). Arrange them in a large roasting pan.

3   In a pestle and mortar, grind together the rosemary, chillies, olive oil, salt and pepper. Pour the mixture over the beetroots and make sure they're evenly coated, mixing with your hands. Roast for 45 minutes, or until golden brown and crunchy.

4   Place the avocado in a bowl with the other guacamole ingredients, mashing together until well combined. Serve alongside the beetroot chips.

YOU WILL NEED

4 beetroot/beets
4 sprigs of rosemary, leaves picked (i)
2 red chillies
75ml/2½fl oz/⅓ cup olive oil
salt and pepper

FOR THE GUACAMOLE

2 avocados, cut into chunks
¼ red onion, finely chopped
handful of fresh coriander/cilantro
juice of 1 lime
salt and pepper

NOTE

i   Other herbs such as thyme and oregano would work well here too.

Herbed Potatoes

with a cashew cheese sauce

serves 8
cooking time: 25 minutes

There is something so comforting about the humble potato. Potatoes seem to have developed a bad reputation of late, but they actually have a number of health benefits. They are high in magnesium and vitamin C, reduce inflammation, enhance immunity and promote digestion.

Cashews and sunflower seeds made me fall in love with creamy plant-based sauces.

METHOD

1 Parboil the potatoes in a pan of boiling salted water for about 10 minutes until soft but still firm in the centres. Drain and pat dry.

2 Heat some oil in a cast iron pan on a medium heat and toss in the potatoes. Don't be tempted to move them too soon. After about 5–7 minutes, turn the potatoes over and cook the other side until golden, another 5–7 minutes. Remove from the heat and add the chopped herbs, salt and pepper.

3 Place all the sauce ingredients except the water in a high-speed blender and gradually add the water until you get a beautiful thick creamy sauce, adding more water as needed for your desired consistency.

4 Serve the potatoes with the cashew cheese sauce generously spooned over the top.

NOTE

i Quick soak the cashews in boiling water for 15–30 minutes.

YOU WILL NEED

8 potatoes, quartered
6 tbsp olive oil
handful of fresh parsley, chopped
couple of sprigs of thyme, leaves
    picked and roughly chopped
couple of sprigs of rosemary, leaves
    picked and roughly chopped
salt and pepper

FOR THE CASHEW CHEESE SAUCE

300g/10½oz/1 cup cashew nuts,
    soaked or sunflower seeds, toasted
    (i)
palm-sized piece of yellow pepper
1 tsp mustard
1 tsp nutritional yeast
salt and pepper
2 tbsp lemon juice
75ml/2½fl oz/⅓ cup water (or more
    as needed)

Rostis

with sweet potatoes and cumin

serves 2
cooking time: 15 minutes

I love these rostis because you can use many different veggies with the same delicious outcome. Potatoes, courgettes/zucchinis, butternut squash, beetroot/beets and carrots all work really well.

Rostis are such a great alternative to bread. Lather with your favourite hummus, some pesto, slices of tomato, fresh greens and some chilli and you've got the perfect stack. Try adding different spices and some chopped-up herbs for added flavour and nutrition.

METHOD

1 Soak the chia seeds in the water for 10 minutes until it forms a gel.

2 Squeeze out any excess water from the grated sweet potato, then combine in a bowl with the rest of the ingredients, except the coconut oil.

3 Heat the coconut oil in a large frying pan on a medium heat. Fry spoonfuls of the rosti mixture until golden brown, about 5 minutes on each side, flattening the rosti out with the back of a spoon.

4 Serve with your favourite toppings.

YOU WILL NEED

1 tbsp chia seeds

75ml/2½fl oz/ ⅓ cup water

1 medium sweet potato/potato, grated, or your vegetable of choice

½ onion, diced

1 garlic, diced clove

thumb-sized piece of root ginger, diced

1 tsp toasted cumin seeds

65g/2¼oz/½ cup chickpea flour

pinch of Himalayan salt and black pepper

1 tsp coconut oil

351

Roasted Turmeric Aubergine/Eggplant

with coriander seeds

serves 4
cooking time: 30 minutes

These crispy aubergine/eggplant chunks are coated in turmeric and other spices and cooked until golden and slightly crunchy on the outside, yet soft on the inside. Try serving them with the BBQ Sauce on page 62, Ginger & Turmeric Sauce on page 46, Peanut Dipping Sauce on page 72 or Black Sesame Tahini on page 76.

YOU WILL NEED

2 large aubergines/eggplants, cut into chunks
pepper
2 tsp ground turmeric
I tsp chilli powder
I tbsp cumin seeds
I tbsp coriander seeds
2 tbsp coconut oil, melted

METHOD

1   Preheat the oven to 220°C/425°F/Gas 7.

2   Arrange the aubergine in an ovenproof dish or baking pan and toss with the spices and oil. Season with pepper, then bake for 30 minutes.

3   Serve with your choice of sauces.

352

JOURNAL ENTRY//

To walk somewhere in your dreams and then set foot upon that ground. How easily our dream and waking lives blur into one beautiful cacophony of parallel worlds. Intuition exists at the core of our souls; if we just take the time to come home (into our bodies and out of the egoic mind), we open our hearts to infinite wonder and magic...

Leh, Ladakh, India, shot on a Panasonic GH4 with a fixed 50mm lens

Hasselbacks

stuffed sweet potatoes with cashew mustard cream

serves 1
cooking time: 45 minutes

This is a delicious potato recipe that can be made with very minimal preparation time and then left in the oven to do its thing.

Sweet potatoes are full of incredible nutrients such as beta-carotene, which is responsible for significantly increasing levels of vitamin A in our blood. Sweet potato cyanidins, peonidins and other colour-related phytonutrients act as heavy metal reducers and anti-inflammatories in the human body.

METHOD

1 Preheat the oven to 200°C/400°F/Gas 6.

2 Make thin slices along the sweet potato without cutting all the way through. (iii) Arrange the sweet potato slices in a roasting tin, drizzle with olive oil, sprinkle with salt and pepper, then stuff the thyme leaves (or your herb of choice) between the slices. Bake for 45 minutes–1 hour until the potato skin is crispy and the flesh is soft.

3 Add the sundried tomatoes and walnut pieces between the slices and return to the oven for the last 1 minute.

4 For the cashew mustard cream, blend all the ingredients in a food processor until smooth and creamy. Drizzle over the potatoes and serve.

NOTES

i   You can substitute this for rosemary, sage or oregano if you'd prefer.

ii   Quickly soaked in freshly boiled water for 15–30 minutes. You can substitute the cashews for macadamias, almonds, sunflower seeds or sesame seeds.

iii A good trick for this is to put two wooden spoons across the top and bottom of the potato, then as you slice down, the knife hits the wood instead of cutting through the potato.

YOU WILL NEED

1 sweet potato per person (depending on size)

olive oil

salt and pepper

couple of sprigs of thyme (i)

2 sundried tomatoes, chopped

small handful of walnuts per person, chopped

FOR THE CASHEW MUSTARD CREAM

small handful of cashew nuts (ii)

juice of 1 lemon/lime

1 tsp mustard

75ml/2½fl oz/⅓ cup warm water

1 tbsp nutritional yeast (optional)

salt and pepper, to taste

Sri Lankan Green Beans & Tomato

with healing spices

serves 4
cooking time: 15 minutes

I love the simplicity of this traditional Sri Lankan dish. It takes only 15 minutes to prepare and cook and is a fresh and tasty side dish. I was always amazed by the variety of vegetable curries cooked traditionally in Sri Lanka – each one intricately spiced, beautifully balanced and made with wonderful local fruits and veggies.

METHOD

1   Heat the coconut oil in a high-sided frying pan on a medium heat and fry the spices until fragrant, about 3-4 minutes. Add the onion and garlic and sauté until golden, about 5 minutes.

2   Throw in the tomatoes, beans, lemon juice and water. Simmer for 5–7 minutes until the sauce thickens.

3   Add salt and pepper to taste and serve.

YOU WILL NEED

1 tbsp coconut oil

1 tsp ground turmeric

1 tsp red chilli powder

1 tsp mustard seeds

1 tsp cumin seeds

1 onion, finely chopped

2 garlic cloves, chopped

4 tomatoes, diced

4 handfuls of green beans, cut into bite-sized chunks

juice of 1 lemon/lime

250ml/9fl oz/1 cup water

salt and pepper

Roasted Chickpeas/ Garbanzo Beans

serves 4
cooking time: 1 hour

These crunchy bites of spicy goodness are one of my favourite staples. They are quick to make and high in protein. I use them in salads, bowls, soups, stews or on roasted veg. For a quick alternative, use canned chickpeas/garbanzo beans rather than dried.

METHOD

1   If using dried chickpeas/garbanzo beans, rinse and drain the soaked chickpeas and place in a saucepan. Cover with water and cook on a high heat until soft but still with a bite, about 45 minutes–1 hour. If using canned, skip this step.

2   Drain and rinse the chickpeas and pat them dry. Transfer them to a frying pan on a medium heat. Toss the spices through, drizzle with oil and season with salt and pepper. Fry for around 15 minutes, or until golden brown. Alternatively grill/broil on high until golden brown and crispy, around 15 minutes.

NOTE

i   Or 2 x 400g/14oz cans of chickpeas/garbanzo beans, drained and rinsed.

YOU WILL NEED

525g/1lb 3oz/3 cups dried chickpeas/
   garbanzo beans, soaked overnight
   (i)
1 tsp ground turmeric
1 tsp ground cumin
1 tsp ground coriander
1 tsp red chilli flakes
2–4 tbsp olive/avocado/coconut oil
salt and pepper

For the Sweet Tooth

The sweet treats in this chapter are all raw – they require no baking and are pretty much fool proof. I always keep some Medicinal Truffles (see page 367) in the fridge to reach for when my sweet tooth hits – they are nutritious, sugar-free and loaded with medicinal adaptogens. For something a little fancier, try the Strawberry Cashew Cheesecake on page 381 or the Raw Carrot Cake on page 378. The beauty of these recipes is that they are actually good for you and you can eat them with gratitude and without the guilt that so often accompanies indulging in something sweet.

Chocolate

with nuts, nut butter and coconut

makes 1 bar
prep time: 10 minutes

This is your chance to make your own delicious chocolate that is highly nutritious. High-quality raw cacao is one of the most beneficial sources of magnesium and acts as an antioxidant. This recipe is a guide for you to fulfil your own cravings! Some combinations I love are: cashew coconut, sea salt and almond, dried fruit and nut, orange zest and walnuts.

METHOD

1   Melt the coconut oil and cacao butter in a saucepan on a low heat. Add the sugar and stir for 1–2 minutes until the sugar has dissolved.

2   Remove from the heat and add the nut butter, cacao, salt and any of your chosen additions. Mix well.

3   Pour into a chocolate mould or spread the mixture out thinly on a baking sheet lined with greaseproof/wax paper. Place in the fridge until hard.

NOTES

i   If you don't have cacao butter, you can use another spoonful of coconut oil.

ii   Or you can use agave or 2–3 dates blended with a touch of warm water.

iii   You can use any of the following: cacao, almond, coconut, cashew or peanut.

YOU WILL NEED

1 tsp coconut oil
1 tbsp cacao butter (i)
1 tbsp coconut sugar (ii)
1 tbsp nut butter (iii)
1 tbsp raw cacao
pinch of salt

OPTIONAL TOPPINGS

nuts, coconut, dried fruit, flowers, herbs
spices like cinnamon, cardamom, nutmeg, chilli
1 drop ingestible essential oil such as peppermint/cardamom/cinnamon

Medicinal Truffles

with nut butter and adaptogens

makes 10–20
prep time: 20 minutes

These truffles are heavenly. I love how chocolatey and amazing they are, but you could easily add a mashed banana or avocado to the mix to increase the variety of nutrients in these balls.

This recipe is simply a guide, so do experiment with your own medicinal ball combinations, such as cashew, date and coconut; apricots, turmeric and walnuts; or rose, vanilla and almond.

Add your favourite adaptogen (see page 25) for a boost in the morning, a gentle pick-me-up in the afternoon, or a calming treat in the evening.

METHOD

1 Pulse the coconut, the dates and then the nuts separately in a food processor until fine.

2 Combine all the ingredients including your favourite optional extras in a bowl, mixing well.

3 Roll into balls and place in the fridge for 30 minutes or the freezer for 15 minutes until firm. You can also roll your balls into more cacao or coconut for added deliciousness.

NOTE

i   Add a combination of these adaptogens and healing spices to really enhance the nutritional benefits of these truffles.

YOU WILL NEED

100g/3½oz/1 cup desiccated/dried
   shredded coconut
150g/5½oz/1 cup nuts of your choice
handful of pitted dates
2 tbsp coconut oil, melted
2 tbsp nut butter
2 tbsp cacao
pinch of salt
1 tsp vanilla extract

OPTIONAL EXTRAS (i)
1 tsp reishi mushroom powder
1 tsp maca
1 tsp moringa
1 tsp ashwagandha
1 tsp ground turmeric

367

Banana Balls

with nuts and healing, balancing adaptogens

makes 10–20
prep time: 10 minutes

You know that banana bread you grew up eating? These banana balls have all the flavour of banana bread but in an amazing energy ball, with nutrients that lift your mood. They're perfect for satisfying that sweet craving after something savoury. They are a great treat for children, and they'll have fun making them too.

I first made these in Sri Lanka, where coconuts were plentiful, and I was always craving that extra bit of energy before or after a long surf.

METHOD

1   Pulse the oats, coconut and nuts in a food processor until fine.

2   In a bowl, mash the bananas, then add the coconut oil, agave or maple syrup, vanilla, cinnamon and a pinch of salt.

3   Combine the wet ingredients with the dry ingredients.

4   Roll into balls and place in the fridge for 30 minutes or the freezer for 15 minutes until firm.

NOTE

i   Add a combination of these adaptogens and healing spices to really enhance the nutritional benefits of these balls.

YOU WILL NEED

100g/3½oz/1¼ cup rolled oats
100g/3½oz/1¼ cup fresh brown
    coconut/dried coconut chips
150g/5½oz/1 cup nuts of your choice
2 ripe bananas
2 tbsp coconut oil, melted
1 tbsp agave/maple syrup
1 tsp vanilla extract
1 tbsp ground cinnamon
pinch of salt

OPTIONAL EXTRAS (i)

1 tbsp cacao powder
1 tsp reishi mushroom powder
1 tsp maca
1 tsp moringa
1 tsp ashwagandha
1 tsp ground turmeric

Mini Cheesecakes

with blueberries, walnuts, a cacao base and maca chocolate topping

serves 8
prep time: 15 minutes

These individual cheesecakes are a creamy dream. The kiddies will love them too and they're filled with nutrients from the blueberries, walnuts, cacao and maca.

Maca is an adaptogen that is good for hormone balancing, increased energy and vitality.

METHOD

1 Line a muffin pan with muffin liners/cases.

2 Blitz together the walnuts, cacao, coconut sugar and coconut oil in a food processor and press the crumbs into the bottom of the muffin molds to make the base of the cheesecakes.

3 Combine all the blueberry filling ingredients in a high speed blender until smooth and creamy. Spoon on top of the bases and then place in the freezer to firm up, around 15 minutes.

4 For the chocolate topping, melt the coconut oil and stir in the remaining ingredients.

5 Pour over the blueberry layer and return to the freezer for a further 15 minutes until the chocolate topping is set.

NOTE

i Quick soak the cashews in boiled water for 15–30 minutes for easier blending.

YOU WILL NEED

125g/4½oz/1 cup walnuts
2 tbsp cacao powder
2 tbsp coconut sugar
2 tbsp coconut oil

FOR THE BLUEBERRY FILLING

150g/5¼oz/1 cup cashew nuts, soaked overnight (i)
250ml/9fl oz/1 cup coconut cream
1 tbsp agave/coconut treacle/maple syrup
handful of blueberries
1 tsp vanilla extract

FOR THE CHOCOLATE TOPPING

2 tbsp coconut oil
1 tbsp cacao powder
pinch of salt
1 tsp maca powder
1 tbsp agave

The Taj Mahal, India, shot on a Panasonic GH4 with a fixed 50mm lens

Raw cupcakes

with chocolate cheesecake topping and coconut biscuit base

serves 8
prep time: 15 minutes

These raw cupcakes are so tasty and very simple to make. They are great to have on hand as an afternoon treat or after-dinner pick-me-up. These are similar to raw cheesecakes but I've called them cupcakes as they have a thicker base layer and thinner, icing-like topping.

METHOD

1   Line a muffin pan with muffin liners/cases.

2   Pulse the walnuts, dates and coconut in a food processor until crumbs form. Add the coconut oil, coconut sugar and salt and pulse again.

3   Spoon the biscuit base mixture into the muffin molds, pressing firmly down.

4   Blend the filling ingredients in the high speed blender until smooth and creamy. Spoon over the biscuit bases.

5   Place in the freezer to set for around 15 minutes until the chocolate topping is set.

NOTES

i   Any nuts or oats also work great.

ii   If you're pressed for time, quick soak for 15–30 minutes in boiling water.

YOU WILL NEED

125g/4½ oz/1 cup walnuts (i)
100g/4oz/½ cup pitted medjool dates
100g/3½oz/1¼ cup dried coconut chips
2 tbsp coconut oil
2 tbsp coconut sugar
pinch of sea salt

FOR THE FILLING

225g/8oz/1½ cups cashew nuts, soaked overnight (ii)
juice of 1 small lemon/lime
2 tbsp agave/maple syrup/coconut treacle
2 tbsp cacao powder
1 tsp vanilla extract
75ml/2½fl oz/⅓ cup coconut milk/ almond milk/water

Creamiest Ice Cream

with banana and beetroot/beet and a homemade cacao sea salt sauce

serves 2
prep time: 15 minutes

Don't be afraid of vegan desserts. Once you have made them, you will realize just how easy and healthy they really are, and you will love them for ever. Frozen banana gives this ice cream its beautiful, creamy texture. If you'd like to experiment with other fruits, use 3 frozen bananas as a base and then a handful of frozen fruit such as berries, pineapple or mango.

METHOD

1. Blend all the ice cream ingredients, along with any optional extras, in a food processor or blender on high until smooth and creamy, adding more nut milk if necessary.

2. For the chocolate sauce, melt the coconut oil, then add the rest of the ingredients and mix well.

3. Pour the chocolate sauce over the ice cream and place in the freezer for 15 minutes to set.

NOTES

i   This recipe works beautifully with other frozen fruits too.

ii Or a small piece of raw beetroot/beet.

iii Add a combination of these adaptogens and healing spices to really enhance the nutritional benefits of these ice cream bowls.

YOU WILL NEED

FOR THE ICE CREAM

4 bananas, cut into chunks and frozen (i)

1 tsp beetroot/beet powder (ii)

1 tbsp nut butter

75ml/2½fl oz/⅓ cup nut milk (or more as needed)

FOR THE CHOCOLATE TOPPING

2 tbsp coconut oil

1 tbsp cacao powder

1 tsp vanilla extract

1 tbsp agave/coconut sugar

pinch of sea salt

OPTIONAL EXTRAS (iii)

1 tsp reishi mushroom powder

1 tsp maca

1 tsp moringa

1 tsp ashwagandha

1 tsp ground turmeric

Raw Carrot Cake

with vegan cream cheese icing and lime zest

serves 4
prep time: 1 hour

This carrot cake is so healthy you could eat it for breakfast. Packed with nutritious proteins, pineapple and carrots, it is moreish, light and delicious. This recipe idea was first given to me by an old friend, which I then adapted and spiced up a bit.

METHOD

1 In a high speed blender, pulse the dates and coconut oil until fine. Spoon into a large mixing bowl, and combine with the rest of the ingredients for the cake. Using your hands here works best to really get everything mixed together.

2 Line a cake pan and press half the mixture into the pan and place in the freezer for around 20–30 minutes until firm.

3 Blend the icing ingredients in the high speed blender until fine and creamy. Spread half the icing onto the first layer of the cake.

4 Press the rest of the cake mixture on top of the icing layer and finish off with the rest of the icing.

5 Dust with cinnamon and coconut and freeze until firm, around 45 minutes.

NOTES

i For oat, coconut or nut flour, you can simply grind your oats, coconut or nuts in a food processor until fine.

ii Preferably overnight, or quick soaked for 15–30 minutes in boiling water.

YOU WILL NEED

FOR THE CAKE

240g/8½oz/1½ cup pitted dates

1 tbsp coconut oil

130g/4½oz/1 cup oat/coconut/
    almond flour (i)

1 carrot, grated

2 slices of pineapple, blended into
    pulp

thumb-sized piece of root ginger,
    grated

1 tbsp ground cinnamon, plus more
    for dusting

1 tsp allspice

100g/3½oz/1 cup desiccated/dried
    shredded coconut, plus more for
    dusting

handful of walnuts, roughly chopped

FOR THE CREAM CHEESE ICING

280g/10oz/2 cups cashew nuts/
    macadamia nuts, soaked (ii)

juice and zest from 1 lemon/lime

1 tbsp coconut oil

2 tbsp agave/honey

1 tsp vanilla extract

250ml/9fl oz/1 cup coconut cream

Strawberry Cashew Cheesecake

with an almond cacao crust

serves 4–6
prep time: 15 minutes

The combination of bitter, raw cacao nibs and sweet fresh strawberries is the best thing about this dessert. I love how creamy the cashews are when blended. Top with more cacao nibs and dried edible flowers.

METHOD

1 For the crust, pulse all the ingredients until fine in a food processor.

2 Line a cake pan and press this mixture into the pan and place in the freezer for 10–15 minutes to firm up.

2 For the filling, combine all the ingredients in a blender until smooth and pour over the crust.

3 Place the cake in the freezer for 30 minutes, or until firm. Remove from the freezer before serving to soften. Add more cacao nibs and dried edible flowers as garnish before serving

NOTE

i Preferably overnight, or quick soaked for 15–30 minutes in boiling water.

YOU WILL NEED

FOR THE CRUST

150g/5½oz/1 cup flaked/sliced
    almonds
55g/2oz/⅓ cup cacao nibs, plus extra
    to garnish
100g/3½oz/⅔ cup coconut sugar
pinch of salt
100g/3½oz/½ cup pitted dates
2 tsp melted coconut oil

FOR THE FILLING

140g/5oz/1 cup cashew nuts, soaked
    (i)
150g/5¼oz/1 cup strawberries
250ml/9fl oz/1 cup coconut cream
squeeze of lemon/lime juice
edible flowers, to garnish

Cataviña, Baja California Sur, shot on a Panasonic GH4 with a fixed 50mm lens

Chia Pudding

with blueberry, cardamom and coconut

serves 1
resting/chilling time: overnight

Chia pudding makes a great breakfast – prepare it the night before and wake up to the most delicious creamy breakfast dessert.

Chia was revered by the Aztecs as a powerful food of the gods. This tiny high-protein seed has a vast array of health benefits and contains omega-3 fatty acids, iron, fibre and is rich in antioxidants.

METHOD

1 Pour the milk into a glass and add the cardamom and chia. Stir and add the rest of the ingredients.

2 Place in the fridge overnight.

3 In the morning, top with fresh or dried coconut slices and blueberries.

YOU WILL NEED

125ml/4fl oz/½ cup coconut milk

½ tsp ground cardamom

3 tbsp chia seeds

1 tsp agave/maple syrup/coconut treacle

½ tsp ground cinnamon

handful of fresh or dried coconut chips, plus extra for serving

handful of blueberries, plus extra for serving

1 tsp lime zest

Avocado Chocolate Mousse

with layers of cashew cardamom cream

serves 4
prep time: 15 minutes

This was one of the first raw desserts I ever made, and everyone went nuts about it! My mum still talks about "Sammy's chocolate avocado mousse" even though I keep saying I did not come up with the concept. It works so beautifully because of the silky, creamy texture of ripe avocados. I promise you won't taste the avocados at all.

Cacao is a superfood and literally acts as a vehicle for carrying nutrients to your cells. Cacao is different from cocoa, which is heated at high temperatures and sadly loses much of its nutritional value.

METHOD

1 For the cashew cardamom cream, put the cardamom pods in the water and soak for 10 minutes. Remove the pods and combine the water with all the other ingredients in a blender on high until smooth and creamy.

2 Blend all the ingredients for the chocolate mousse on high until smooth and creamy.

3 Alternate layers of the chocolate mousse and cashew cream in your serving glasses.

4 Place in the fridge for 30 minutes or the freezer for 15 minutes until the mousse hardens. Garnish with a generous dusting of cacao over the top and toasted almonds.

NOTE

i Quick soak the cashews in boiled water for 15–30 minutes for easier blending.

YOU WILL NEED

FOR THE CASHEW CARDAMOM CREAM

6 cardamom pods
60ml/2fl oz/¼ cup water
140g/5oz/1 cup cashew nuts, soaked (i)
1 tbsp coconut oil
1 tbsp agave/coconut treacle
250ml/9fl oz/1 cup coconut cream
juice of ½ lemon/lime

FOR THE CHOCOLATE MOUSSE

4 avocados
250ml/9fl oz/1 cup coconut cream
1 tbsp coconut oil
2 tbsp agave/coconut treacle
3 tbsp cacao powder, plus extra to garnish
1 tsp vanilla extract
pinch of salt
handful of almonds, toasted, to garnish

Raw Brownies

with cacao, coconut and dates

serves 6
prep time: 25 minutes

These brownies are made with only 4 ingredients, take 2 minutes to whip up and 20 minutes to set in the freezer.

The texture is exactly like the most chocolatey, moist brownie you've ever eaten. I promise that you will make these again and again! I make this even more decadent by adding a rich chocolate sauce, which is totally optional as these are equally delicious without it.

METHOD

1 If you're using fresh coconut, pulse in a food processor until fine. Transfer to a bowl.

2 Pulse the dates, cacao and coconut oil with a pinch of salt. Mix in the coconut by hand, massaging everything together. Press the mixture into a square 18x12½cm/7x5in lined tin or dish baking pan, then place in the freezer until firm, usually around 20 minutes.

3 Combine all the sauce ingredients until smooth and creamy.

4 Remove the brownies from the freezer and pour the chocolate sauce over the top (if using). Cut into pieces and serve.

NOTES

i   If you can, get the fresh brown coconut; otherwise desiccated is better.

ii If you don't have coconut butter, use any other nut butter.

YOU WILL NEED

100g/3½oz/1 cup fresh coconut or desiccated/dried shredded coconut (i)
240g/8½oz/1½ cup pitted dates
60g/2¼oz/½ cup cacao powder
2 tbsp coconut oil
pinch of salt

FOR THE CHOCOLATE SAUCE (OPTIONAL)

1 tbsp coconut treacle or agave
2 tbsp coconut milk
2 tbsp cacao powder
1 tbsp coconut butter (ii)

Cacao Cashew Pie

with rose, bougainvillea and a date coconut crust

serves 6
prep time: 35 minutes

Although this pie looks fancy, it is incredibly simple. It requires no cooking and can be made in 15 minutes, popped in the freezer for 20 minutes and you've got this moreish creamy chocolate ganache filling with a seriously chewy, crust that tastes like salted caramel.

METHOD

1 For the crust, pulse the dates in a food processor, transfer to a bowl and then add the coconut oil and dry ingredients, mixing with your hands. Press the mixture into a round pie dish lined with baking parchment.

2 In a blender, combine the filling ingredients until smooth and creamy. Spoon on top of the crust.

3 Place in the freezer until firm, about 20 minutes. Remove from the freezer to soften before serving with dried rose and bougainvillea petals.

NOTES

i   I make my own by pulsing the oats or nuts in a food processor until fine.

ii Preferably overnight, or quick soaked for 15–30 minutes in boiling water.

iii Or 3 tablespoons of cacao powder.

YOU WILL NEED

handful of dried rose and bougainvillea
    petals, to garnish

FOR THE CRUST

240g/8½oz/1½ cup pitted dates
2 tbsp ground cinnamon
1 tbsp coconut oil, melted
100g/3½oz/1 cup desiccated/dried
    shredded coconut
pinch of salt
90g/3¼ oz/¾ cup nut/oat flour (i)

FOR THE FILLING

280g/10oz/2 cups cashew nuts,
    soaked (ii)
1 tbsp coconut oil
100g/3½oz slab of sugar-free vegan
    dark chocolate, melted (iii)
2 tbsp coconut treacle/agave
250ml/9fl oz/1 cup coconut milk
thumb-size piece of root ginger
pinch of salt

Playa Maderas, Nicaragua, shot on a Nikon D90, with a 18–55mm lens

Rituals & Meditations

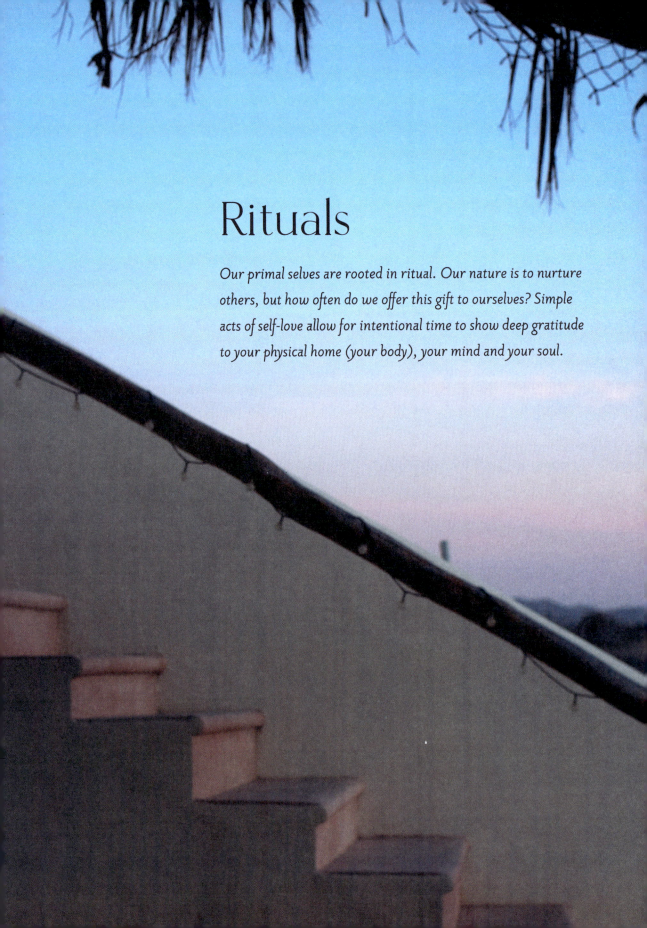

Rituals

Our primal selves are rooted in ritual. Our nature is to nurture others, but how often do we offer this gift to ourselves? Simple acts of self-love allow for intentional time to show deep gratitude to your physical home (your body), your mind and your soul.

Hot oil self massage

The benefits of practicing self massage on a daily basis are incredible, from improving circulation and self esteem to regulating lymph flow and detoxing. To do this use the oil of your choice, such as coconut or olive, a few drops of your favourite essential oils and gently warm the oil by placing it in a container in a bowl of hot water. This should be done either before or after a shower. Massage the oil into your skin starting from the head, all the way down to the toes. Get to know your body and take this time to thank every part of it in this beautiful act of self-love. Self massage stimulates a general feeling of calm and wellbeing.

Herbal steams

Harvest herbs you have in your garden or choose your favourite essential oils. Boil the kettle and pour the water into a saucepan and grab a towel. Add the herbs/essential oils to the pan and cover with the towel. Sit somewhere comfortable with the pan on a table or on your lap, with the towel covering your head to keep the steam in. Essential oils are very concentrated and can be incredibly strong, so it's not necessary to use more than 1-2 drops of each oil. Put some relaxing music on and breathe…

Herbal bath

Choose your favourite plants from your garden – remember to double check if you are not sure whether something is usable. Amazingly, most plants (unless toxic) have wonderful qualities that you may never have known or expected Some of my favourites include:

Geranium: balances hormones and alleviates cramps
Rosemary: anti-spasmodic properties for muscle aches and pains, improves circulation
Lavender: calming and anti-septic
Lemon/lime leaves: removes stale energy and uplifts mood
Rose petals: soothes irritated skin, brightens complexion and tightens pores
Chamomile: relaxing and calming
Bougainvillea: anti-septic and detoxifier, relieves joint pain and stomach ache
1 cup Epsom salts/coarse sea salt: draws toxins out of the body and eases pain and cramping
A couple drops of **essential oils** of your choice
2 tbsp olive oil for drier skin

Herbal smudge sticks

Harvest rosemary, lavender and sage and bundle them together tightly using string. Hang to dry for a couple of days and use to smudge your home, clothing and car. This involves burning the herbs to cleanse a space with the smoke. Smudge all four corners of a room and the doorway to get rid of old energy and make space for new, fresh flow.

Tongue scraping

When we sleep our tongue releases toxins which form a thick coating. A stainless steel or copper tongue scraper should be used to remove this coating from the tongue first thing in the morning. This prevents unwanted toxins from re-entering the body. If you don't have a tongue scraper, a teaspoon works perfectly.

Oil pulling

One tablespoon of coconut oil or sesame oil swished around the mouth for 5-10 minutes directly after tongue scraping aids in the removal of unwanted toxins. Coconut oil has anti-septic properties that improve gum and teeth health and naturally whitens the teeth considerably.

Sacred lunar infusion

Choose the flower with your favourite scent. Sit with the plant and ask for its flowers for healing purposes. Gently pick the flowers and place in a bowl of spring water. Leave them under the moon for a night. Remove the flowers from the water with a sieve/fine-mesh strainer and bottle up the water. Use as a room, linen, mist or space clearer and even as a face toner. This ritual fosters a deep connection with the plants that grow around you. Infusing spring water with the essence of these plants harnesses their healing properties.

Baja California Sur, shot on a Sony a6500 with a Mitakon Zhongyi fixed 35mm lens

For what is it to die but to stand naked in the wind and melt into the sun?
And what is it to cease breathing but to free the breath from its restless
tides, that it may rise and expand and seek God unencumbered?

Only when you drink from the river of silence shall you indeed sing.
And when you have reached the mountaintop, then you shall begin to climb.
And when the earth shall claim your limbs, then shall you truly dance.

Khalil Gibran - The Prophet

Healing Mantra

Sa Ta Na Ma

Translated as: Infinity, life, death, rebirth.

This is the cycle of life.

400

The sounds come from the Sanskrit phrase SAT NAM, meaning Truth is my Identity.

The mantra should be repeated in three different "voices":

» The singing voice - action.

» The whispered voice - the inner mind or your romantic nature.

» In silence where you repeat the mantra mentally to yourself - your spiritual voice.

As you repeat the chant, bring together your thumb and a specific finger so they touch in this order:

1 **Sa:** thumb and index finger – the mudra for wisdom connected to the planet Jupiter.

2 **Ta:** thumb and middle finger – the mudra for patience connected to the planet Saturn.

3 **Na:** thumb and ring finger – the mudra for energy connected to the planet Uranus.

4 **Ma:** thumb and little finger – the mudra for communication connected to the planet Mercury.

Studies have shown that this mantra is effective in increasing the flow of serotonin in your brain, reducing anxiety and stress, improving the quality of your sleep, enhancing focus, memory and promoting emotional healing.

Rio Celeste, Costa Rica, shot on a Pentax k1000 with a fixed 35mm lens

Your Body is a Temple

Have you ever told your body you love each unique part of it? What if we taught our children to thank their body parts every day for their magic? Our bodies are incredibly sensitive and intelligent, responding to thoughts and feelings just as humans, plants and animals do.

I spent so much of my life focusing on the parts of my body I did not like, from my arms that were too fat, to the rolls on my tummy that I couldn't stand, to my massive breasts which eventually resulted in breast reduction surgery.

When did you last say thank you to your hands, for example? Or your feet, or legs that have carried you miles through this lifetime? Your voice that has allowed you to speak your truth or your heart that has pumped blood through your veins?

During my three-month trip through India, I was introduced to this idea of the body responding incredibly quickly to the thoughts of the mind. Every evening after my shower, I self massaged

coconut oil into every part of my body, thanking it and asking for its forgiveness for never having done so before (a daily self massage is a principle of Ayurveda).

The results were astounding and rapid. By the time my trip was over, my body had responded in the most incredible way, toning and tuning to the love I was sending it by changing the way I thought and doing yoga every day or every other day.

I made use of the beautiful affirmation from ho'oponopono (an ancient Hawaiian healing system) that suggests that every situation we encounter in life is a response to our own actions and thoughts.

Please forgive me
I'm sorry
Thank you
I love you

Here's some questions to ask yourself:

» Do you treat your body as your temple?

» Do you shower each part of it with love?

» Do you nourish your body with high vibrational foods?

» Do you cleanse and detox your body when it feels good to do so?

» Do you self-massage, dry brush, use Epsom salt baths or perform gentle stretches?

» Do you offer yourself and your body kind and loving words?

» Do you give your body the time to reset in nature?

» Do you adorn your body with natural fibres that are free from toxins and harsh chemicals?

If you don't, that's ok. The body is very forgiving and heals quickly. Start now. Start again. We all ebb and flow and it's ok to do so, but if your body is crying out for your love and attention, don't ignore it. If you ignore the cries, they become screams. We can harness the power of preventative medicine now before disease arises.

Kasol, Himachal Pradesh, Northern India, shot on a Panasonic GH4 with a fixed 50mm lens

CBD Oil

Place equal parts CBD flowers to coconut oil in a glass jar with the lid lightly screwed on, placed on low heat in a double boiler/bain marie for 24–48 hours to infuse. Make sure you grind the flowers until fine in a coffee grinder or food processor. Alternatively you can cook the combination of the CBD and coconut oil on the lowest heat possible in a cast iron pot on the stove for around 12-24 hours. Strain the flowers from the oil and store the oil a glass jar. At this point you can add a couple of drops of essential oil like peppermint for a delicious flavour and uplifting quality.

My experience growing cannabis changed my life forever. I always knew that there was something out there that I was yet to find that would complete me, make me understand my purpose and feel connected in a deeply gratifying way. This plant, along with yoga, was my healer and allowed me to stay off of chemical anti-depressants when dealing with grief, giving me space to grieve and mourn, but also to be held in doing so, taking the edge off of the darkest days.

My connection to cannabis grew deeper as I learned how to plant, grow and nourish her, water and love her. And just as she had taken care of me, in a magical reciprocity, I was able to nurture her and share her healing with others. Like any natural substance with incredible power and potential, prohibition results in misunderstandings of its usage and purpose and subsequent bad experiences with this medicinal plant. As we move out of the age of Pisces which was governed by war, conflict and the ego and into the Age of Aquarius, the rise of the divine feminine perfectly coincides with the freedom of cannabis, a female plant. I have used this medicine for anxiety, grief, pain relief, focus, concentration, sleep and more.

There is something incredibly magical about (re)connecting with the earth and returning to our source. Growing organic, medicinal cannabis for two years gave me a strong desire to help ensure that this plant is given the understanding, love and recognition it so deserves. We all have the ability to be our own healers and growing your own plant medicine is a very powerfully healing process in itself.

Where THC is powerful for pain, CBD is incredible for inflammation and more often than not, a specific ratio of CBD to THC is what is required in order to treat certain ailments more efficiently. My CBD coconut oil recipe is made with organic, sun-grown CBD flowers and virgin cold pressed coconut oil.

JOURNAL ENTRY //

We arrived in the dark, the smell of smoke still lingering in the air as we pulled to a stop in the emerald green van. It felt like we'd climbed continuously on our drive, through winding forest roads. This place felt strangely familiar to me, like I had been there before. It vibrated with a sense of possibility and excitement, despite the fires that had raged through these lands just days before, devouring everything in their path. I always dreamed I would meet and explore you, California.

*Calaveras County, California, shot on a
Pentax k1000 with a fixed 35mm lens*

Index

Samantha is a holistic chef, recipe developer, photographer, writer and yoga instructor. After majoring in English and Photojournalism, she travelled the world for 10 years and now calls The Garden Route, South Africa, home.

She wrote, styled and photographed all of the recipes, journal entries and travel photographs in this book, making her the single contributor to this food and travel journal, which documents her plant-based food journey.

Sam spends her days creating. Inspired by nature, elemental living and the healing power of plants, she dreams of owning her own piece of land upon which to grow food and medicine and to welcome others to heal in nature.

Find her here:
www.samanthadormehl.com
Instagram @samanthadormehl